THE HUNTING & FISHING LIBRARY®

By Dick Sternberg

DICK STERNBERG has fished for every major trout and salmon species, pioneering some of the Great Lakes techniques popular today. He formerly directed the salmonid research program for the Minnesota DNR.

PARKER BAUER has worked as a trout guide in Yellowstone National Park and has written many films and magazine articles on trout and salmon. He's fished for stream trout from Montana to New York, and from British Columbia to Labrador.

BEN STREITZ, an accomplished fly fisherman, conducts numerous fly-casting seminars and builds custom fly rods. He spent several years guiding for trout, salmon and grayling on the premier streams of southwest Alaska and Kodiak Island.

CY DECOSSE INCORPORATED
Chairman: Cy DeCosse
President: James B. Maus
Executive Vice President: William B. Jones

TROUT
Author and Project Director: Dick Sternberg
Editor: Parker Bauer
Art Directors: Bradley Springer, William B. Jones
Project Manager: Tracy Holte
Technical Advisors: Parker Bauer, Ben Streitz
Consultant: Tom Helgeson
Principal Photographer: William Lindner
Photo Directors: Joseph Cella, Ben Streitz
Contributing Photographers: Joel Arrington; Frank Balthis; Hiliary Bates; Erwin and Peggy Bauer; Randy Binder/Minnesota Department of Natural Resources; Joseph Cella; Bob and Clara Calhoun/Bruce Coleman, Inc.; Mark Emery; Ted Fauceglia; Bob Firth; Jeff Foott; David H. Funk; Calvin Gates; John Goplin; Daniel Halsey; Tracy Holte; Paul Horsted/South Dakota Tourism; David L. Hughes; Spike Knuth/Virginia Department of Game and Inland Fisheries; Mark Macemon; Mark Miller; Jack Olson/Colorado Department of Natural Resources; The Orvis Company, Inc.; Buzz Ramsey; Lynn Rogers; Mark Romanack; Stephen Ross; William Roston; Ron Schara; Dick Sternberg; Ben Streitz; University of Washington Fisheries Institute; Jeffrey Vanuga/OVIS; Yukio Yamada
Illustrators: Maynard Reece, Jon Q. Wright
Researchers: Robert Merila, Ben Streitz, Mike Hehner, Jim Moynagh, Eric Lindberg
Production Manager: Jim Bindas
Assistant Production Manager: Julie Churchill
Typesetting: Kevin D. Frakes, Linda Schloegel, Jennie Smith
Production Staff: Janice Cauley, Sheila DiPaola, Joe Fahey, Carol Kevan, Yelena Konrardy, Scott Lamoureux, Bob Lynch, David Schelitzche, Nik Wogstad
Cooperating Individuals and Agencies: The American Museum of Fly Fishing; Joel Anderson; Atlantic Salmon Federation — Alex T. Bielax; Bright Waters, Inc. - Tom Helgeson; Simon Brooks; Larry and Kathy Brunner; Burger Brothers Sporting Goods — John Edstrom, Kelly Ferguson, John Goplin, Greg Lonke, Scott Schumacher; California Department of Fish and Game - John M. Deinstadt, Jim Ryan; Colorado Division of Wildlife - Bill Weiler; Colorado State University - Dr. Robert Behnke; Brian Cummings; D & G Bait Company; Dan Bailey's Fly Shop - John Bailey, Dan Lahren; Bill Davis; Dusty Joe and Jimmy Finley; Fisheries and Oceans of Canada Pacific Biological Station - Dr. J.R. Brett, Dr. Cornelius Groot; Jed Flanagan; Tom Fleming; Butch Furtman; George Anderson's Yellowstone Angler - Chris Cauble; Jamie Goldsmith; Dave Goulet; Mike Hayworth; Bill Hill; Bud Hodson; Bruce Hovland; Idaho Fish and Game Department - Al Van Vooren; Intermountain Research Station, Forest Service - Bill Platts; Jack Sokol & Associates, Inc.; Carl Jones; Hugo and Ruby Kettula; Richard Kirchner; Lefty Kreh; T.J. Laviolette; Dave Lucca; Maryland Department of Natural Resources - Dr. Robert Bachman; Karl Maslowski; Brian McKinly; Bob Mead; Michigan Department of Natural Resources - Bill McClay; Minnesota Department of Natural Resources - Randy Binder, Larry Gates, Mel Haugstad, Gerald Johnson, Steve Oie, Duane Shodeen, Ed Stork; Greg Muecke; New Brunswick Department of Natural Resources and Energy - Allen Madden; Newfoundland and Labrador Department of Development and Tourism - Len Rich; Nova Scotia Tourism and Culture - Bill Brison; Jim and Rob Nygard; Ontario Ministry of Natural Resources - Jack Imhof; Oregon Department of Fish and Wildlife - Rich Berry; Pennsylvania Fish Commission - Richard Snyder; Quebec Ministry of Leisure, Fish and Game - Yvon Cote; R & R Marine; Arron Richardson; Mike Snyder; S.P.A.W.N. (Newfoundland) - Rick Squire; Sports North, Yukon Territories - Glen Babala; Norm and Sil Strung; Thorne Brothers - Tom Anderson; Trout Unlimited; Vermont Department of Fish and Wildlife - Rod Wentworth; Bob White; Wyoming Game and Fish Department - John Baughman; Dennis Zwirlein

Cooperating Manufacturers: Berkley, Inc.; Columbia Sportswear Company; Daiwa Corporation; Feldmann Eng. & Mfg. Co., Inc.; Fenwick/Woodstream; G. Loomis, Inc.; Glacier Gloves/Swan Enterprises, Inc.; Goold Mfg.; Interphase Technologies; Johnson Fishing, Inc.; Koden International, Inc.; La Crosse Footwear, Inc. - Doug Jorgenson; Lamiglass, Inc.; Lowrance Electronics - Steve Schneider, Allan Tarvid; Luhr Jensen & Sons, Inc. - Roger Newfeldt, John Thomas; Martin Reel Company; Mercury Marine/Mariner Outboards - Stan Bular, Jim Kalkofen, Clem Koehler; Micronar Electronics/Hondex Marine Electronics - Jack Phillips; Nordic Crestliner Boat Co. - Del Smith; Normark Corporation; The Orvis Company, Inc. - Hiliary Bates, John Harder, Tom Rosenbauer; Pflueger Fishing Tackle; Plano Molding Company - Bill Cork; Rainbow Lure Co.; Sage/Winslow Mfg. Corp.; Scientific Anglers/3M - Jean Kohn; Simms/Life-Link Intl.; Sunline Company, Ltd.; Uncle Josh Bait Company - Gene Berce; Wave Wackers/Herrick Enterprises.

Printer: Times Printers Pte. Ltd. (1293)

Also available from the publisher: *The Art of Freshwater Fishing, Cleaning & Cooking Fish, Fishing With Live Bait, Largemouth Bass, Panfish, The Art of Hunting, Fishing With Artificial Lures, Walleye, Smallmouth Bass, Dressing & Cooking Wild Game, Freshwater Gamefish of North America, Fishing Update No. 1, Secrets of the Fishing Pros, Fishing Rivers & Streams, Fishing Tips & Tricks, Fishing Natural Lakes, White-tailed Deer, Northern Pike & Muskie, America's Favorite Fish Recipes*

Contents

Introduction

In stream-trout fishing, versatility is the key to success. Trout streams undergo dramatic changes over the course of the year, and no single technique can be expected to work all the time.

In spring, when heavy rains and snowmelt cause streams to run high and muddy, fly fishing is tough. But you can still catch trout by spinfishing with small plugs, spinners and spoons. If the water is exceptionally muddy, live bait may be the only answer. When the streams subside and the water clears, trout feed heavily on insects and fly fishing yields good results.

But despite the obvious arguments for versatility, most trout-fishing literature promotes specialization. In fact, some fly-fishing books now deal with only one aspect of the sport, like nymphing. These narrow-scope books have their place, but are of little value to the angler who wants to become a well-rounded trout fisherman.

Regardless of whether your interests lie more in fly fishing or in spinning, this book will show you how to catch stream trout under a wide range of conditions. We start by helping you understand trout behavior. You'll learn how trout detect danger, find food, select cover, and react to changes in weather.

Then, we'll give you a concise course on selecting stream-fishing equipment, including fly rods, lines and leaders, spinning and baitcasting tackle, and even drift boats. We'll show you how to stock your fishing vest and how to choose a good pair of waders.

The fly-fishing section starts with complete instructions for rigging your tackle properly, something that too many fly fishermen don't do. Every important fly-fishing tactic is presented using a no-nonsense approach. The basic fly casting techniques are demonstrated with clear photos that make each step easy to understand, even for a beginner. You'll learn the most productive ways to fish dry flies, wet flies, nymphs, streamers and special-purpose flies.

The spinning and baitcasting section details everything from the basic casting, trolling and drift-fishing techniques, to new methods such as jigging, to time-proven tactics like freelining with live bait. And if you're not into fly casting, we'll show you how to use flies with spinning tackle. After you learn all the best ways to catch trout, we'll give you instructions on the right way to release them so you can do your part to insure quality fishing in years to come.

A section on special situations will help you catch trout under conditions that cause big problems for many stream-trout anglers. You'll learn the tricks that help experts catch lots of trout in high water or low water, in heavy cover, at night, and even in winter. We'll also reveal the secrets of catching trophy trout.

Completing the book is a roundup of the top North American trout streams. We'll give you our top picks on regional maps, along with pertinent information on the type of stream, species present and the exact reach that offers the best fishing.

This book is much different from other trout-fishing books you've read. It doesn't try to convert you to a particular style of fishing, it lacks the elitist overtones so apparent in many books, and it won't confuse you with reams of meaningless details. What it will do is help you catch a lot more trout.

Understanding Trout & Salmon

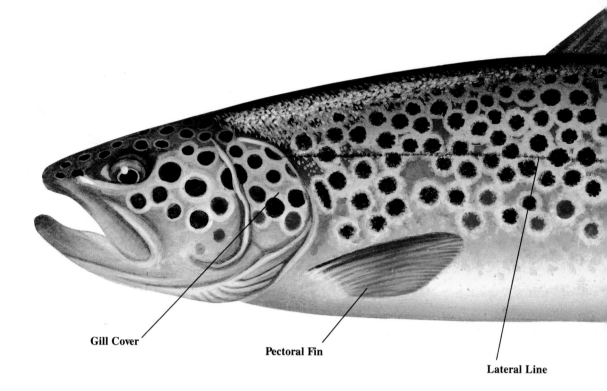

Gill Cover

Pectoral Fin

Lateral Line

Trout & Salmon Basics

Trout and salmon have long been considered superior gamefish, the ultimate in wariness and fighting ability. In years past, many anglers regarded them as the only true gamefish.

Unfortunately, this wary nature has led to the popular notion that the fish are superintelligent, and therefore extremely difficult for the average angler to catch. But there is no evidence to indicate they are more intelligent than other gamefish species.

The notion is reinforced when anglers see feeding trout being "put down" by even the slightest movement or vibration. But this instinctive reaction should not be confused with intelligence. Like any other fish, trout become conditioned to flee for cover to avoid predators. As soon as they hatch, trout face attacks from predatory insects, crayfish and small fish. As they grow older, they are attacked by larger fish and by kingfishers, herons and other predatory birds. Most stream fishermen have seen dead trout along the bank with gaping beak wounds in their heads. The wariness of trout also results from natural selection; those that lack wariness do not live to reproduce.

What distinguishes trout and salmon from other gamefish is their preference for cold water. Although temperature preferences vary among trout and salmon species, most seek water temperatures from 50° to 65°F, and avoid temperatures above 70°. This requirement means they can live only in streams or lakes fed by springs or snowmelt, or in lakes with deep, unpolluted water.

Trout and salmon belong to the family *Salmonidae*. Besides trout and salmon, the family includes grayling, found mainly in Alaska, the Yukon and the Northwest Territories, and whitefish, which are widely distributed in the northern states and Canada but have minor importance to anglers.

For the purposes of this book, the term "trout" includes not only true trout (genus *Salmo*), but also chars (genus *Salvelinus*). True trout, such as browns and rainbows, have dark spots on a light background; chars, such as brook trout and Dolly Varden, have light spots on a dark background. Chars require colder water than true trout.

Atlantic salmon are closely related to true trout and belong to the same genus, *Salmo*. Pacific salmon belong to a different genus, *Oncorhynchus*, meaning "hooknose." Pacific salmon spawn only once, dying soon afterward; other members of the family may live to spawn several times. All salmon species are *anadromous*; they spend their lives at sea, then return to freshwater streams to spawn. Salmon stocked in freshwater lakes spawn in lake tributaries.

Many species of trout, including rainbow, brook, brown and cutthroat, have anadromous forms with a different appearance than the forms limited to fresh water. The anadromous forms are generally sleeker and more silvery.

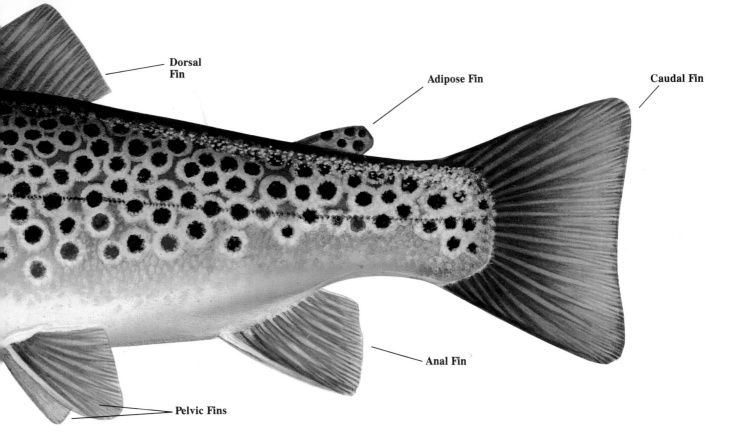

Dorsal Fin

Adipose Fin

Caudal Fin

Anal Fin

Pelvic Fins

Powerful fighters, trout and salmon have remarkable stamina. Some species, like rainbow trout and Atlantic salmon, leap repeatedly when hooked; others, like brook trout, wage a deep, bulldog-style battle. Most trout and salmon are excellent eating, but there is a growing trend toward catch-and-release fishing. In some heavily fished waters, catch-and-release is mandatory. It has long been the accepted practice for Atlantic salmon because the species is so rare and so treasured as a gamefish. Catch-and-release fishing insures that the fish remain in a stream long enough to spawn and produce "wild" progeny. The other alternative, frowned upon by most trout enthusiasts, is put-and-take stocking of hatchery-reared trout.

To become a successful trout or salmon fisherman, you must shed the notion that there is an aura of mystery surrounding these fish. Although they live in prettier settings than most other fish, they have the same behavior patterns and the same needs for food and cover. Learn to think of their basic needs and you will have no trouble finding them. Learn to approach them stealthily, like a predator, and you will have no trouble catching them.

Identification Key to Major Salmonid Groups

Start with the pair of pictures marked *1*. It will identify the group or send you to another pair.

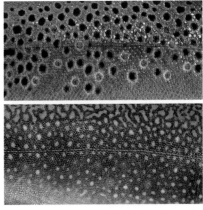

1 Dorsal fin longer than head . . . . .
GRAYLING

Dorsal fin shorter than head . . . . . go to 2

2 Anal fin longer than deep . . . . . .
PACIFIC SALMON

Anal fin no longer than deep . . . . . go to 3

3 Dark spots on light background . . .
TROUT AND ATLANTIC SALMON

Light spots on dark . . . . . CHARS

Stream-Dwelling Trout & Salmon

Practically all North American species of trout and salmon can be found in streams at some time of the year. Even lake-dwelling trout swim into streams in spring or fall to spawn. Only the lake trout, a species not covered in this book, spawns primarily in lakes. Following are brief descriptions of the trout and salmon species that stream fishermen are most likely to encounter.

Trout and Atlantic Salmon

COMMON RAINBOW TROUT *Salmo gairdneri gairdneri*

All rainbows have radiating rows of black spots on tail, black spots on back and sides, and no teeth on tongue. Common rainbows have pinkish horizontal band and pinkish gill cover with some black spots. World record: 27 lbs., 3 oz.; Ganaraska River, Ontario; 1984.

COASTAL RAINBOW TROUT (steelhead) *Salmo gairdneri irideus*

Body longer and sleeker than that of common rainbow; fewer spots below lateral line. Steelhead may have faint pinkish horizontal band and gill cover, but gill cover has few or no black spots. World record: 42 lbs., 2 oz.; Bell Island, Alaska; 1970.

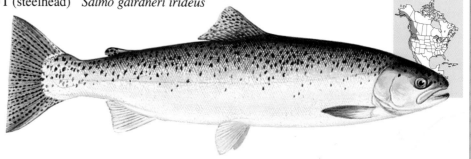

BROWN TROUT *Salmo trutta*

Square tail with few or no spots; adipose fin (arrow) with some spots. Sides light brownish to yellowish with black spots and usually some red or orange spots. Spots often have whitish to bluish halos. World record: 35 lbs., 15 oz.; Lake Nahuel Huapi, Argentina; 1952.

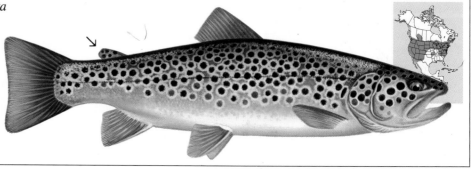

YELLOWSTONE CUTTHROAT TROUT *Salmo clarki bouvieri*

All cutthroat have reddish slash marks on throat, black spots on tail, and patch of teeth at base of tongue. Yellowstones have spots above and below lateral line; spots are more concentrated toward rear. No official record.

COASTAL CUTTHROAT TROUT *Salmo clarki clarki*

Sides and back heavily spotted; spots uniformly distributed from front to rear. Background color more silvery than that of other subspecies of cutthroat, and reddish slash marks on throat may be faint. No official record.

WEST SLOPE CUTTHROAT TROUT *Salmo clarki lewisi*

Spots on West Slope cutthroat are even more concentrated toward rear than those on Yellowstone cutthroat. But the spots are somewhat smaller, and usually absent on front half of body below lateral line. No official record.

GOLDEN TROUT *Salmo aguabonita*

Golden sides with reddish horizontal band that runs through about 10 dusky, oval-shaped marks. Tail spotted. Dorsal, pelvic and anal fins with white tips. World record: 11 pounds; Cook's Lake, Wyoming; 1948.

ATLANTIC SALMON *Salmo salar*

Sides silvery to yellowish brown. Like brown trout, Atlantic salmon have few or no spots on tail. Tail slightly forked rather than square. Adipose fin unspotted; adipose of brown spotted. World record: 79 lbs., 2 oz.; Tana River, Norway; 1928.

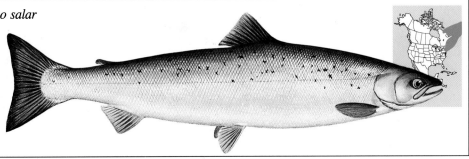

Grayling

ARCTIC GRAYLING *Thymallus arcticus*

Dorsal fin with base at least as long as fish's head; fin has rows of blue or violet spots. Pelvic fins with light streaks. Sides violet-gray and silver with small dark spots. World record: 5 lbs., 15 oz.; Katseyedie River, N.W.T.; 1967.

Chars

BROOK TROUT (speckled trout) *Salvelinus fontinalis*

Background color brownish to greenish. Back laced with light, wormlike marks; sides have light spots and some red spots, both with blue halos. Lower fins with white leading edges. World record: 14 lbs., 8 oz.; Nipigon River, Ontario; 1916.

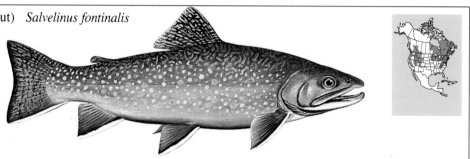

ARCTIC CHAR *Salvelinus alpinus*

Background color silvery green. Sides with pinkish, reddish or cream-colored spots, some at least as large as pupil of eye. Lower fins with white leading edges. World record: 32 lbs., 9 oz.; Tree River, N.W.T.; 1981.

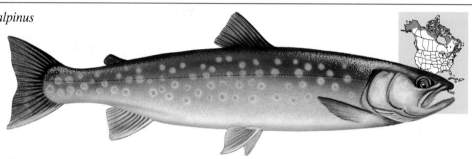

BULL TROUT *Salvelinus confluentus*

Sides silvery green to dark green with pinkish to whitish spots. Lower fins with white leading edges. Head considerably longer, broader and more flattened than that of Dolly Varden. World record: 32 lbs.; Lake Pend Oreille, Idaho; 1949.

DOLLY VARDEN *Salvelinus malma*

Silvery green sides with pinkish, reddish or whitish spots. Lower fins with white leading edges. Resembles Arctic char and bull trout, but spots smaller than char's, and head less flattened than bull's. World record: 10 lbs., 2 oz.; Kenai River, Alaska; 1985.

Pacific Salmon

CHINOOK SALMON (king salmon) *Oncorhynchus tshawytscha*

Sides silvery; upper sides, back, and both lobes of tail peppered with small black spots. Teeth set in blackish gums. Anal fin, usually with 15 to 19 rays, is longer than that of other Pacific salmon. World record: 97 lbs., 4 oz.; Kenai River, Alaska; 1985.

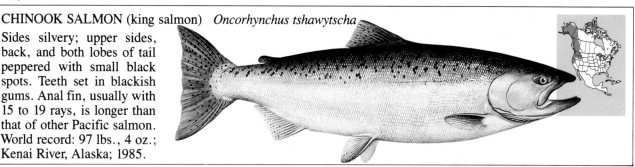

COHO SALMON (silver salmon) *Oncorhynchus kisutch*

Resembles chinook, but tail with small black spots on upper lobe only. Teeth set in whitish to grayish gums. Anal fin considerably shorter than that of chinook, usually with 12 to 15 rays. World record: 31 lbs.; Cowichan Bay, British Columbia; 1973.

PINK SALMON (humpback salmon) *Oncorhynchus gorbuscha*

Sides silvery; upper sides, back and entire tail with large black spots, some as large as eye. Spots on back, sides and tail of chinook much smaller than eye. World record: 12 lbs., 9 oz.; confluence of the Moose and Kenai rivers, Alaska; 1974.

SOCKEYE SALMON (red salmon) *Oncorhynchus nerka*

Silvery sides with brilliant bluish to greenish back, often with black speckles. Tail unspotted. Resembles chum salmon, but lacks the faint vertical bands. World record: 12 lbs., 8 oz.; Situk River, Alaska; 1983.

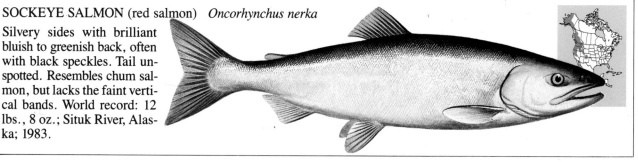

CHUM SALMON (dog salmon) *Oncorhynchus keta*

Sides silvery, often with black speckles on the back but no distinct black spots. Faint vertical bands on the side intensify as spawning time nears. Tail unspotted. World record: 32 lbs.; Behm Canal, Alaska; 1985.

13

Senses

Stream fishermen know that a sudden movement, a heavy footstep, a shadow or a fly rod glinting in sunlight will send a trout scurrying for cover. Salmonids depend mainly on vision to detect danger, but they also have an excellent sense of smell and a well-developed lateral-line sense.

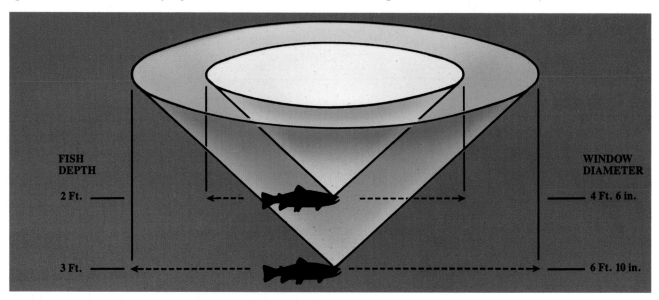

FISH DEPTH

2 Ft.

3 Ft.

WINDOW DIAMETER

4 Ft. 6 in.

6 Ft. 10 in.

VISION. When approaching salmonids, remember that they can view the outside world clearly through a "window," a circular area on the surface whose size depends on the depth of the fish. The diameter is slightly more than twice as wide as the fish is deep. A trout at a depth of 2 feet would have a window 4 feet, 6 inches wide. Surrounding the window, the surface is a mirror, so the fish can't see out.

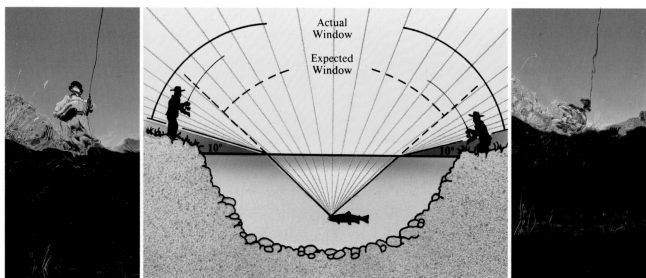

Actual Window

Expected Window

10°   10°

Light rays entering a trout's window are bent, so the above-water field of vision is larger than you would expect. Rays near the edge of the window are bent and compressed most, so objects at a low angle are highly distorted. Light rays in the middle of the window aren't bent at all, so objects at a high angle appear almost normal. If you stand upright and stay just outside the expected window of vision, the trout will clearly see your upper body (left photo). If you crouch at the same distance from the trout, you will be less visible because your image is so distorted (right photo). If you stay low enough, less than 10 degrees above the edge of the window, you will be completely hidden from view.

14

Many frustrated fishermen can attest to the fact that salmonids have excellent color vision. A lime-green spoon may produce fish after fish, but a similar Kelly-green spoon will not draw a strike. Because the fish are so color-selective, anglers often paint their lures at streamside or apply colored tape in an attempt to determine the color of the day.

Trout and salmon have only fair night vision. With the exception of large brown trout, they do little feeding after dark. And even browns seem to have difficulty locating a fly unless it produces noise or vibration.

SMELL. Trout and salmon use their sense of smell to find food, avoid predators and locate spawning areas. If you drop a gob of fresh salmon eggs in a clear pond filled with rainbows, the eggs will "milk" as they sink, leaving a scent trail. Feeding trout mill about until they cross the trail, then they turn and follow it to the eggs.

Researchers in British Columbia found that salmon turned back from their spawning run and headed downstream when a bear was fishing upstream of them. The salmon detected a chemical emitted by

the bear called L-serine. This chemical is also given off by human skin.

Salmon and migratory forms of trout navigate at sea or in large lakes by using the sun, currents and the earth's magnetic field. These clues enable them to return to the vicinity of their home stream at spawning time. Once they get this far, they rely on scent to find the right stream. Amazingly, they can return to the exact area of the stream where their lives began. When researchers cut a salmon's olfactory nerves, it could not find its way back.

Biologists have discovered that they can dramatically increase the percentage of chinook salmon returning to a given stream by "imprinting" the young fish before they move to open water. Just as the young start to smolt (p. 27), a chemical that can be detected in extremely low concentrations is dripped into the stream. The smell of this chemical somehow gets locked into the fish's memory. Then, when the salmon reach maturity, the same chemical is again dripped into the stream. In some cases, this technique has doubled the return rate.

LATERAL LINE. Veteran stream fishermen step very lightly when wading the streambed or walking the bank, even when outside the fish's field of vision. And they realize that vibration-producing lures work better in murky water or after dark than lures that produce little vibration. The fish evidently detect footsteps and lure vibrations with their lateral-line system, a network of ultra-sensitive nerve endings along the side of the body.

ALASKA

Netting sockeyes at sea.

Sockeyes spawning in small tributary.

NORTHWEST
TERRITORIES

BRITISH
COLUMBIA

Driftwood R.

Forfar Cr.

ALBERTA

Fraser R.

Gulf of Alaska

Fraser R.

N

*Pacific
Ocean*

100   200   300

ONE INCH EQUALS 200 MILES

- - - - - - SOCKEYE MIGRATION ROUTE

WASHINGTON

MIGRATION PATTERNS of Pacific Salmon have been revealed by tagging studies. Sockeyes netted in the Gulf of Alaska migrated 1300 miles to the mouth of the Fraser River. Tagged fish have been found as far as 650 miles upstream, spawning in Forfar Creek. Sockeyes have been seen even farther upstream, in the Driftwood River, 730 miles from the Fraser's mouth. From their starting point in the Gulf, these fish traveled more than 2000 miles.

Feeding & Growth

During their early years, trout and salmon feed mainly on immature forms of aquatic insects and to a lesser extent on adult insects, both aquatic and terrestrial. They also eat small crustaceans, molluscs and earthworms. As they grow larger, they continue to eat a lot of insects, but small fish make up an increasing percentage of their diet. Large trout do not hesitate to eat small animals like frogs and mice. Some salmon species, such as sockeye and pink, are plankton feeders, filtering tiny organisms from the water with their closely spaced gill rakers. This feeding behavior makes them very difficult to catch on hook and line.

Dolly Varden have gained an unenviable reputation as predators on the eggs and young of other trout and salmon. In years past, Alaska paid a bounty on Dollies, and hundreds of thousands were taken with nets, spears and explosives as well as hook and line. There is no denying that Dolly Varden will eat the eggs and young, but research has shown that most of the eggs eaten have drifted from the redd and stand little chance of hatching. In truth, practically all trout and salmon will eat the eggs and young of other species, and of their own kind, when the opportunity presents itself.

How fast a trout grows depends not only on the type of food it eats, but also on the fertility and size of the stream.

Generally, trout that feed primarily on insects grow more slowly than those that eat lots of small fish; insect-feeding consumes more energy for the amount of nutrients obtained. Trout in mountain streams usually grow slower than those in farm-country streams. These high-altitude streams are colder and less fertile, so they produce considerably less food. Brown trout, for instance, seldom exceed 1 pound in small mountain streams where insects are the major food. But they grow to 15 pounds or more in rivers with marginal temperatures for trout but with plenty of baitfish.

Trout that live in small brooks have a slower growth rate than those in good-sized rivers because the bigger water offers a greater abundance and diversity of foods. The size of the spawning stream seems to affect the size of chinook salmon, even though the salmon do very little feeding in the stream. The Chilkotin River, a tributary of the Fraser River in British Columbia, has a flow of only 7 cubic feet per second; the Chilko River, another tributary, has a flow of 80 cfs. Chilkotin salmon average about 25 pounds and top out at 40; Chilko salmon average 35 pounds and top out at 60.

Genetics also affects growth rate. Fast-growing strains of many species have evolved naturally or have been produced by fish culturists who select and breed the fastest-growing individuals from each year-class. Donaldson rainbow trout, a strain selectively bred for fast growth at the University of Washington, may reach 10 pounds in only 2 years, provided they have enough food. A normal rainbow of the same age weighs less than a pound, even if food is abundant.

Male trout and salmon grow faster than females; salmonids differ in this respect from most other fish species.

Salmonid Diet and Life Span

SPECIES	COMMON FOODS	FEEDING HABITS	MAX. AGE
Rainbow trout	mainly insects; also plankton, fish eggs, small fish, crustaceans	often feeds on surface	11
Brown trout	primarily insects; large browns feed mostly on fish and crayfish	feeds on surface more than other trout; heaviest feeding around dawn and dusk	8
Cutthroat trout	mostly insects and small fish; also fish eggs, crustaceans, frogs	often feeds on surface	9
Golden trout	insects, especially caddisfly and midge larvae; also crustaceans	often feeds on surface	7
Brook trout	mainly insects and small fish; diet extremely varied	not as selective as most other trout; feeds on surface at times	15
Bull trout	mainly fish; also insects, molluscs, crustaceans	not prone to surface feeding	19
Dolly Varden	mainly small fish and fish eggs; also insects	often feeds behind migrating salmon, eating their eggs	19
Arctic char	small fish, fish eggs, insects, plankton	mainly subsurface feeders, but may feed on floating insects	40
Arctic grayling	mainly insects and fish eggs; also small fish, molluscs, crustaceans	often feeds on surface	10
Pink salmon	plankton, crustaceans, squid, small fish	does not feed in streams, but occasionally take baits and lures	normally 2, up to 3
Chinook salmon	mostly fish; also shrimp, squid, crustaceans	does not feed in streams, but strikes baits and lures	normally 4, up to 9
Coho salmon	mainly fish; also crustaceans	does not feed in streams, but strikes baits and lures	normally 3, up to 5
Chum salmon	plankton, small fish, squid, crustaceans	does not feed in streams, but may take baits and lures	normally 4, up to 7
Sockeye salmon	mostly plankton and small crustaceans; also small fish and bottom organisms	does not feed in streams, but occasionally takes baits and lures	normally 4, up to 8
Atlantic salmon	crustaceans, insects and small fish	does not feed in streams, but will rise to flies out of reflex	14

STONEFLY nymphs crawl up on a streamside object prior to hatching. Then (1) the nymphal case begins to split down the back, (2) the wings and legs of the adult begin to appear and (3) the adult crawls away from the

Common Stream Insects

In their quest to "match the hatch," some fly-fishing enthusiasts spend endless hours studying stream insects and tying flies that closely mimic the real thing. Some experts can identify hundreds of different insect species and tie flies to match. But in most situations, you do not have to duplicate hatching insects so precisely. If you can recognize the insect group and the life stage the trout are feeding on, and then use a fly of about the same size, shape and color, you can catch all but the most selective trout.

Stream insects are grouped into four major orders represented by thousands of species. These orders include mayflies, caddisflies, stoneflies and midges.

Dun

Spinner

Mayfly Nymph

MAYFLIES. Among the most common aquatic insects in eastern and midwestern streams, mayflies are especially abundant in limestone streams and spring creeks. They normally have a one-year life span, most of which they spend as a nymph. Mayfly nymphs are easily recognized by the single pair of wingpads and gills on the upper surface of the abdomen. Most species have three long tail filaments.

When a mayfly nymph matures, it swims to the surface, its skin splits down the back, and a *subimago*

or *dun* emerges. The dun drifts on the surface until its wings dry, and during this time is an easy target for trout. It then flies to streamside vegetation, and after a day or two transforms into a sexually mature adult, or *spinner*. Duns have grayish or brownish upright wings; spinners have clear upright wings, more vibrant colors and longer tail filaments. Mayflies are the only aquatic insects with this two-step adult stage.

STONEFLIES (photos above). These insects abound in the West, especially in cold mountain streams. They will not tolerate pollution or warm water, so they make good indicators of water quality.

Like a mayfly, a stonefly spends most of its aquatic life as a nymph. The nymphal stage lasts from one to four years. Stonefly nymphs have two pairs of wingpads instead of one, two short tail filaments instead of three long ones, and the gills are on the underside of the thorax, rather than the upper surface of the abdomen. Adults are dull-colored, with wings that lie flat against the back.

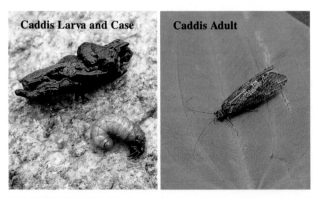

Caddis Larva and Case

Caddis Adult

CADDISFLIES. In the majority of trout streams, caddisflies are the most common aquatic insect. They are more tolerant of pollution and warm water than most other aquatic insects. Their life cycle consists of two aquatic stages, the larva and the pupa. The

case. The adult (4) rests on the object until its wings dry. Males drum their abdomen against the hard surface to

attract females. After mating, the females deposit the eggs while running on or flying over the water.

small wormlike larva is cream-colored, with a dark head and three sets of jointed legs near the front of the body. It often lives in a case built from sand grains, twigs or other debris. The cases are commonly attached to rocks. Some larvae roam freely over the bottom, with or without cases. These are the ones most often eaten by trout.

After about a year, the larvae seal themselves into cases to pupate. The cases are usually attached to a rock or other object. Inside the cases, the pupae develop legs and wingpads. After a few weeks, they chew through their cases, crawl out and dart for the surface. There, they transform quickly to adults and fly away. The adults are grayish or brownish, with tentlike wings.

Overall, caddis larvae are much more important as trout food than the pupae or adults. Although trout will eat pupae in their cases, the pupae are most vulnerable as they swim for the surface.

mally, the larvae cling to vegetation or bottom debris. Some burrow into mucky bottoms. A trout may consume hundreds of the tiny larvae each day. After several months, the larvae begin to pupate, but some kinds do not form cases. Instead, they move about actively for about two weeks before maturing and swimming to the surface. The legs of adult midges are long, especially the forelegs, and look quite frail. Trout feed heavily on the pupal and adult forms.

One sure way to find out what a trout has been eating is to pump its stomach. But first, you have to catch a trout. Even with no trout in hand, you can get an idea of their diet by seining with a fine-mesh net or turning over rocks, then examining the clinging insects.

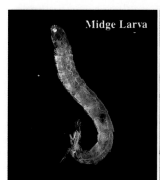
Midge Larva

Midge Adult

MIDGES. This group includes the tiniest aquatic insects. Midges are most numerous in slow-moving, vegetated stream stretches. Like caddisflies, midges have larval and pupal stages.

Midge larvae are more slender than caddis larvae. They do not have jointed legs or live in cases. Nor-

A hatch chart can give you some guidelines on the type of insect likely to be hatching in your region at a certain time of year and time of day. But hatch charts can be misleading because different streams in the same region have different hatches, and hatching times can vary by several weeks depending on the weather. You may be able to get more specific information on hatches in a particular stream by inquiring at a local fly shop.

Understanding the Rise

When a trout or salmon takes a floating insect, the resulting surface disturbance is called a *rise*. A rise can tell you not only where the fish is located, but also what it is eating. Inexperienced fishermen often make the mistake of casting directly to a rise in hopes of catching the trout. But in most cases, the rise occurs well downstream of the trout's lie

How a Trout Takes a Floating Insect

FEEDING TROUT face into the current. They watch the surface closely to spot insects or other food drifting into the window of vision.

After spotting an insect, a trout drifts downstream tail first while carefully examining it. The trout may drift only a foot or two or as much as 25 feet.

Common Rise Forms

SIP RISE. Generally means trout are surface-feeding on mayfly duns or stoneflies. A trout sucks in the insect without breaking the surface. In smooth water you see a ring; in broken water it may not be apparent. Cast a dry mayfly or stonefly imitation well ahead of the rise.

HEAD-AND-TAIL RISE. Usually means the trout is feeding on insects in the surface film. The head appears first; then, as the fish rolls, you see the dorsal fin and finally the tail. Cast a spinner, terrestrial, nymph or midge pupa well upstream of the rise and let it drift naturally.

(see below). To present your fly where the trout is holding, you must cast well upstream of the rise. By watching exactly how trout are rising, you can get an idea of what type of insect they are taking. You may be able to determine the life stage of the insect, the group it belongs to, and possibly the exact species. This information helps you arrive at a strategy for catching the trout. At the bottom of these pages are some of the most common rise forms and what they are telling you:

The trout rises to take the insect, leaving a noticeable ring on the surface. The tendency of most anglers is to cast just upstream of the ring.

Immediately after rising, the trout returns upstream to its lie. If you cast just above the ring, your fly alights too far downstream, behind the trout's window of vision.

SPLASH. The trout completely clears the water, usually to catch emerging insects such as caddisflies or insects dipping in the water to deposit eggs. Use a wet fly, angle your cast downstream, then let the current swing the fly to the trout. Or, skate a caddis dry fly on the surface.

TAILING. Technically, this is not a rise because the fish is not feeding on the surface. When you see a protruding tail, the trout is probably rooting immature insects or scuds from the bottom. Drift a nymph or scud pattern along bottom to the fish.

Spawning Behavior

PHYSICAL CHANGES. Before spawning, trout and salmon, particularly the males, undergo astounding anatomical changes. A male's jaws lengthen and the lower jaw develops a large hook, or kype. Sometimes

Salmonid spawning habits vary greatly among species. Most spawn in fall, but some like the rainbow trout, spawn in spring. Trout, char, grayling and Atlantic salmon live to spawn several times, but Pacific salmon spawn only once, then die. Typically, salmonids require flowing water to spawn, but brook trout and sockeye salmon sometimes spawn in lakes. All but the grayling dig a *redd*, or nest for depositing the eggs. Spawning habits of salmonids are summarized in the chart on page 27.

the upper jaw also becomes hooked, making it impossible for the fish to clamp its jaws together. The teeth of male Pacific salmon grow much larger before spawning, evidently to help them defend their territories (photo below). Male pinks and sockeyes develop a pronounced hump on the back just ahead of the dorsal fin. Their grotesque appearance may also intimidate predators and competing males that approach the spawning site.

Both sexes undergo dramatic color changes. Color shifts are different for different species, but in most cases, the colors become considerably darker and more intense. Color changes are most pronounced in Pacific salmon. As spawning time approaches and their bodies begin to deteriorate, they change from bright silver to brilliant red, olive green or even black.

Normal Male Brook Trout

Spawning Male Brook Trout

SPAWNING SITE. Trout and salmon prefer a clean gravel bottom for spawning, usually at the tail of a pool or in some other area where the current sweeps the bottom free of silt.

The female digs the redd. She turns on her side and beats her tail against the bottom, moving the gravel away and creating a depression longer than her body and about half as deep.

As the female digs, she is often accompanied by more than one male; the largest male is dominant and defends his territory by charging the smaller ones, using his kype to nip them. A female commonly digs several redds, depositing a portion of her eggs in each.

SPAWNING ACT. The dominant male courts the female by nudging and quivering. Finally, the two lie side by side in the redd. They become rigid, arch

their backs, and with their mouths agape, vibrate to release sperm and eggs. Sometimes, the other males also deposit sperm in the redd.

After spawning, the female digs at the upstream edge of the redd, covering the eggs with several inches of gravel. When all spawning activity is completed, the parents abandon the redd. Female Pacific salmon try to guard their redds for a short time, but they soon weaken and die. Salmonids do not attempt to guard the young after they hatch.

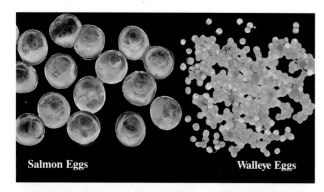
Salmon Eggs   Walleye Eggs

Fry with Attached Yolk Sacs

Parr

EGGS AND INCUBATION. Trout and salmon are less prolific than most other gamefish. They have very large eggs, few in number. A 10-pound rainbow deposits only about 4,000 eggs; a walleye of the same size, for comparison, about 200,000. Salmonid eggs incubate from one to five months, depending on species. This long incubation period subjects the eggs to many hazards, such as disease and flooding. Eggs that are not well-buried are quickly eaten by predators such as crayfish, insects and fish, includ--ing trout.

JUVENILE STAGES. The eggs hatch in the gravel, and at first the fry can move very little. They do not feed, but get nutrients from the attached yolk sac. After several weeks, they gain enough strength to wiggle through the gravel and emerge into the stream. Soon afterward, the fry absorb the yolk sac and begin feeding on plankton.

As the fish grow, they develop a row of dark, oval-shaped marks along the side. At this stage, the fish are called *parr*; the markings, *parr marks*. All species of trout and salmon, except the golden trout, lose their parr marks as they mature.

In the case of anadromous fishes like salmon and steelhead, the young spend at least six months, and sometimes as long as three years, in the home stream before they start to develop migratory tendencies. As the migratory urge develops, the parr marks start to disappear, the sides turn a brilliant silver, and the fish begin moving downstream. This process is called *smolting*, and the young are called *smolts*. The smolts spend several years at sea or in a large lake before reaching maturity.

Smolts

26

Predation is severe during a trout's early life. Kingfishers, herons, otters and fish take the greatest toll. As a rule, fewer than 1 percent of newly hatched fry survive to age 1.

HOMING. Salmon are known for their uncanny ability to return to their home stream to spawn, swimming thousands of miles across oceans and up rivers (p. 17). Trout have the same ability to a lesser extent.

Although migratory salmonids sometimes stray to other rivers, the vast majority return to the same river, and usually to the precise area of the river where they were hatched years earlier.

Where spawning streams have been polluted or blocked by dams, salmon populations decline or disappear because the fish do not seek out alternative streams.

Kingfisher with a Young Trout

When and Where Salmonids Spawn

SPECIES	SPAWNING TEMP. (°F)	TIME OF YEAR	TYPICAL SPAWNING SITE	OTHER
Rainbow trout	50-60	spring	small tributary	steelhead spawns in tail of pool in swift stream
Brown trout	44-48	fall	upper portion of stream or small tributary	
Cutthroat trout	43-47	spring	smallest tributaries	some populations spawn only in alternate years
Golden trout	48-52	midsummer	tails of pools in main stream or tributary	
Brook trout	40-49	early fall	headwaters of stream, often around upwelling springs	occasionally spawns in lakes
Bull trout	45-50	early fall	small tributary	
Dolly Varden	40-45	fall	main channel	eggs must incubate in very cold water
Arctic char	37-41	fall	quiet pool, usually below falls	
Arctic grayling	44-50	early spring	small tributary	does not build a redd
Pink salmon	43-48	fall	lower portion of river	runs are heavier in alternate years
Chinook salmon	40-55	fall	deep riffles in main channel	separate runs in spring, summer and fall
Coho salmon	46-52	late fall	slow-moving tributary or slough	
Chum salmon	45-55	fall	small, slow-moving tributary	
Sockeye salmon	45-52	fall	tributaries to upstream lakes	may spawn along lakeshore
Atlantic salmon	42-50	fall	upper portion of large river system	leaps seemingly impassable falls

Hatchery Trout vs. Wild Trout

To many trout enthusiasts, "hatchery" is a dirty word when coupled with trout. But other trout fishermen realize that without hatchery-reared trout, they would have no trout-fishing opportunities.

There is no denying that hatchery-reared trout lack many of the desirable attributes of wild ones. They are much less wary, and considerably easier for fishermen and predators to catch. Many are caught within a few days of stocking; few make it through the first season. When hooked, they wage a comparatively weak battle and are much less likely to jump. From a fisheries manager's point of view, the "hatchery product" is very expensive, an 8- to 10-inch yearling costing from $.50 to $1.00.

The main gripe against hatchery trout is that they compete for food and space with wild ones. Often, the size and number of trout in a stream increase dramatically when stocking is discontinued. Another problem is genetic contamination. When hatchery trout breed with wild ones, the offspring are normally less suited to the environment than the wild trout were.

Hatchery trout are also inferior on the dinner table. They have white meat, often with a faint liver taste from the pellets they are fed. Wild trout normally have pinkish meat with a tasty salmon-like flavor. For all of these reasons, most natural-resources agencies have reduced the number of trout they stock; on many streams, stocking has been discontinued altogether. The money saved is often spent to improve degraded stream habitat. Unskilled trout fishermen continue to pressure agencies for more hatchery trout, because they find wild ones too difficult to catch. But most serious trout anglers prefer the wild-trout management.

Of course, streams that do not have suitable conditions for natural reproduction must be stocked if there is to be a trout fishery. Managers continue to stock catchable-size trout in many such put-and-take streams, particulary near large cities. But the put-and-take management is gradually giving way to a put-grow-and-take philosophy; the trout are stocked as fry or fingerlings, then allowed to grow up in the stream. This type of stocking is considerably cheaper, and the trout that survive to catchable size bear a much closer resemblance to wild trout.

HATCHERY trout (bottom) are easy to distinguish from wild trout (top). They lack the brilliant coloration of wild trout, and in many cases their fins are badly worn from constant rubbing against concrete raceways.

Habitat

Mention the term "trout stream," and most people think of flowing water that is cold, clear and unpolluted. This stereotype is accurate, but there are other requirements as well. The quantity and size of trout a stream produces depend on the following:

WATER FERTILITY. A stream's fertility, or level of dissolved minerals, affects the production of plankton, the fundamental link in the aquatic food chain. The level of dissolved minerals depends mainly on the water source. *Limestone* streams generally have a considerably higher mineral content than *freestone* streams.

A limestone stream is normally fed by underground springs rich in calcium carbonate, an important nutrient, and flows over a streambed that supplies even more minerals. Limestone streams have more aquatic vegetation, produce more insects and crustaceans, and generally grow more and larger trout.

A freestone stream is fed by runoff or springs with a low mineral content. It typically flows over a streambed that contributes few nutrients to the water. But some freestone streams pick up extra nutrients from fertile tributaries, so they produce good-sized trout. For more details on stream types, see pages 36-37.

WATER TEMPERATURE. All streams that support permanent trout populations have one thing in common: a reliable source of cold water.

The cold water comes from springs, or meltwater from snow or glaciers. Streams fed by ordinary surface runoff become too warm for trout in midsummer, except in the North or at high altitudes, where air temperatures stay cool all year.

Some trout can survive at surprisingly warm water temperatures. Browns and rainbows, for instance, live in streams where temperatures sometimes rise into the low 80s. But at these temperatures, they usually feed very little, their growth rate slows, and their resistance to disease diminishes.

The stream temperature depends not only on the water source, but also on the shape and gradient (slope) of the channel, and the amount of shade.

GRADIENT. The most productive trout streams have a relatively low gradient, from .5 to 2 percent, which converts to 25 to 100 feet per mile. In other words, the streambed drops that many feet for each mile of length. The higher the gradient, the faster the current.

Mountain streams may have a much higher gradient, sometimes as great as 15 percent. Above 7 percent, a stream must have stairstep pools, boulders, log jams or other slack-water areas if it is to support trout.

A channel with a gradient less than .5 percent tends to have a silty bottom and water too warm for trout.

BOTTOM TYPE. A clean gravel or rubble bottom (left photo) produces much more insect life than a sandy or silty bottom (right photo). It also makes a better spawning substrate.

Streambed siltation is a major problem facing many trout streams. Excess silt can result from logging, poor farming practices and overgrazing of stream banks. The silt clogs up the spaces between the gravel, destroying insect habitat and causing eggs deposited in the gravel to suffocate.

Conservation agencies often fence trout streams to keep out cattle, allowing vegetation to redevelop.

Temperature Zones in a Typical Trout Stream

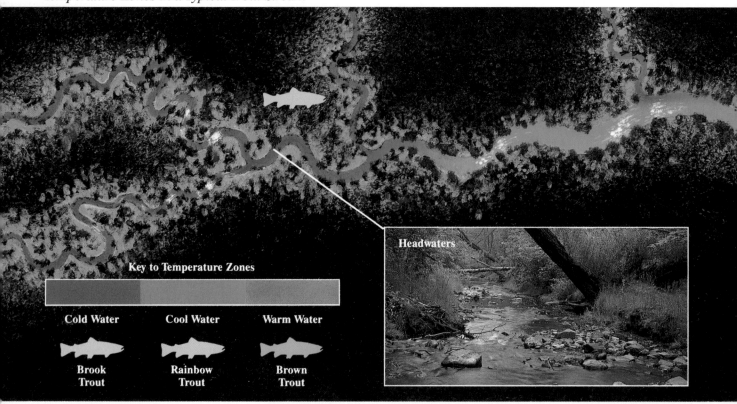

Key to Temperature Zones

Cold Water   Cool Water   Warm Water

Brook   Rainbow   Brown
Trout   Trout   Trout

Headwaters

STREAMS with a distinct cold-water source commonly have temperature zones. The upper zone, or headwaters, normally has very cold water, a low flow, and a narrow streambed. The headwaters serves as a spawning and rear-

ing area, but is too small to support large trout. Because of the cold water, it may hold brook trout. Along the stream course, tributaries flow in, increasing the stream's size. The middle zone has cool water and is the

HABITAT DIVERSITY. A stream with diverse habitat generally produces more trout than one with uniform habitat throughout. Where the habitat is diverse, trout find a variety and abundance of food. Many types of aquatic insects thrive in riffles and runs; baitfish and burrowing aquatic insects abound in pools. If a stream has aquatic vegetation, like stonewort or watercress, the plants often host scuds, midge larvae and other trout foods. Diverse habitat also provides plenty of resting and spawning areas.

Streams that meander in a snakelike pattern (left photo) have greater habitat diversity than streams with a straight channel (right photo). Consequently,

they have more natural cover for trout. As a stream winds along, banks along the outside bends become undercut and tree roots wash out, making ideal hiding spots. Fisheries managers dread the prospect of stream channelization. They know that when the channel is artificially straightened, riffle-run-pool habitat disappears, and trout disappear with it.

SHAPE OF CHANNEL. A narrow, deep channel is generally better than a wide, shallow one. In the latter, a higher percentage of the water is exposed to the air and sun, causing the water to warm more rapidly.

Where the channel is too wide, there is not enough current to keep silt in suspension. So it settles out, smothering gravel beds that provide food and spawning habitat.

Stream-improvement projects are often intended to narrow a channel that has been widened by eroding banks or beaver dams.

STABILITY OF FLOW. Almost any stream can support trout in spring, when water temperatures are cool and flows are high. But trout must live in the stream year around. If the flow falls too low, even for a few days, trout will probably not survive.

Middle Zone

Lower Zone

most productive part of the stream. It has the best insect crop and generally supports the highest population of adult trout, often brooks, browns and rainbows. As more tributaries flow in, the stream gets even larger, and the

streambed flattens out. The water is warm, the current slow and the bottom silty. The lower zone supports few trout, but some of the largest ones. You may find big browns along with suckers, carp and even catfish.

Low flows present the biggest problem in late summer, especially in areas with little forest cover to preserve ground moisture. If the weather is hot and there has been little rain, too much water evaporates from the stream, reducing the depth and slowing the current so the remaining water warms faster. Even if trout survive the warm water, they are under so much stress that they do not feed.

Low water can also be a problem in winter. In a dry year, winter flows may drop so low that the stream freezes to the bottom.

Large underground springs provide the most stability. They insure at least a minimal flow so the stream doesn't dry up during a drought. And because spring water comes out of the ground at the same temperature year around, these streams stay cool in summer and relatively warm in winter.

SHADE. Most streams require some shade from trees or overhanging grasses to keep the water cool enough for trout. A stream that lacks sufficient shade will be cool enough in the upper reaches, but the water will warm rapidly as it moves downstream, so the trout zone is limited. A stream with too much shade may hold trout over most of its length, but the cold temperature inhibits food production and slows trout growth. Fisheries managers have found that they can maximize trout production by planting or removing trees to regulate the amount of shade.

WATER CLARITY. Most trout species prefer clear water, although some, like browns and rainbows, can tolerate low clarity. Clear water allows sunlight to penetrate to the streambed, promoting the growth of plants which in turn produce trout food. Clear water also makes it easy for trout to see food and avoid predators, including fishermen.

DISSOLVED OXYGEN. A lack of adequate dissolved oxygen is rarely a problem in trout streams, unless the water is quite stagnant and high in organic pollutants. In most instances, oxygen is replenished through contact with the air.

pH. In most streams the exact pH level is of little importance to fishermen. Trout, like most fish, can tolerate a wide range of pH levels, and can live in waters with a pH as low as 4.5 or as high as 9.5. But extremely low pH levels resulting from acid rain have wiped out brook trout populations in parts of the Northeast. Many kinds of trout foods, like mayflies, are less tolerant of low pH levels than the trout themselves.

Typical Trout-Stream Habitat

SPRING-FED TRIBUTARIES cool the water below the point where they enter the stream. They attract trout in mid- to late summer.

UNDERCUT BANKS usually form along outside bends. They offer excellent midday cover, especially in sunny weather.

RIFFLES are morning and evening feeding areas. Trout and salmon usually spawn just above or below riffles, but may spawn right in them.

RUNS, the deep, moderately fast-moving areas between riffles and pools, hold trout almost anytime, if there is sufficient cover.

POOLS are smoother and look darker than other areas of the stream. They make good midday resting spots for medium- to large-sized trout.

Habitat Preferences of Salmonids

SPECIES	PREFERRED WATER TEMP (°F)	PREFERRED CURRENT SPEED	OTHER
Rainbow trout	55-60	medium-fast	often strays far from cover to find food
Brown trout	60-65	slow-medium	most cover-oriented of all trout
Cutthroat trout	55-62	medium	thrives in inaccessible waters
Golden trout	58-62	medium	found only in high-altitude waters
Brook trout	52-56	medium	commonly found in cold headwaters
Bull trout	45-55	medium	often found in deep holes
Dolly Varden	50-55	medium	prefers deep pocket water
Arctic char	45-50	fast	usually found near deep water
Arctic grayling	42-50	medium	found along edges of fast current
Pink salmon	52-57	slow	concentrates in lower stretches of river, close to ocean
Chinook salmon	53-57	medium	hangs near bottom in large, deep pools
Coho salmon	53-57	slow-medium	often found in backwaters or eddies
Chum salmon	54-57	medium	swims upstream only to first major barrier
Sockeye salmon	50-55	medium	stays close to bottom in fast water; suspends in pools
Atlantic salmon	53-59	medium	landlocked form found in some streams as well as lakes

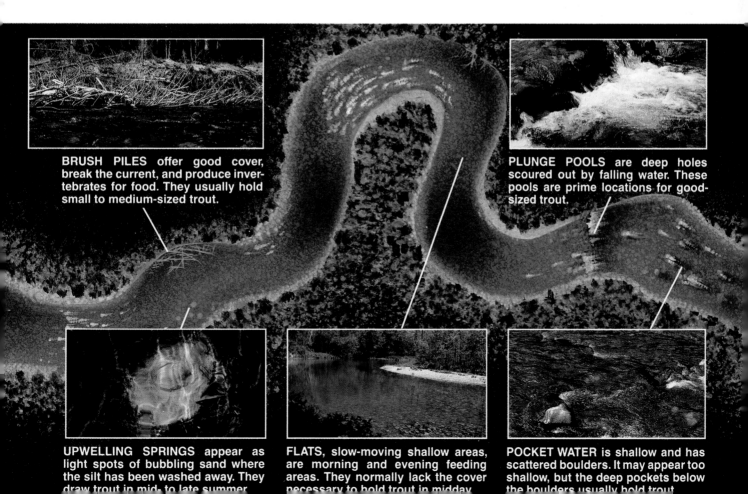

BRUSH PILES offer good cover, break the current, and produce invertebrates for food. They usually hold small to medium-sized trout.

PLUNGE POOLS are deep holes scoured out by falling water. These pools are prime locations for good-sized trout.

UPWELLING SPRINGS appear as light spots of bubbling sand where the silt has been washed away. They draw trout in mid- to late summer.

FLATS, slow-moving shallow areas, are morning and evening feeding areas. They normally lack the cover necessary to hold trout in midday.

POCKET WATER is shallow and has scattered boulders. It may appear too shallow, but the deep pockets below the boulders usually hold trout.

Typical Trout and Salmon Streams

Trout and salmon are found in streams ranging in size from meadow brooks narrow enough to hop across, to major rivers large enough to carry ocean-going vessels. Described below are the most common types of trout and salmon streams, representing both the limestone and freestone categories (p. 31):

Freestone Streams

MEDIUM-GRADIENT FREESTONE streams, the most common trout stream type, have moderate current with numerous pools, riffles and runs. The streambed is comprised mostly of large gravel, rubble and boulders, and has some pocket water (p. 35). Most medium-gradient freestone streams are fed by surface runoff and meltwater.

Because the water carries few nutrients, these streams are relatively unproductive. But many have large tributary systems which add enough nutrients to produce abundant food and large trout. The best of these streams have good spring flow, keeping water temperatures in the ideal range for trout feeding and growth.

HIGH-GRADIENT FREESTONE streams, fed by snowmelt and surface runoff, are usually found in mountainous areas. The current is fast, with long stretches of pocket water but few pools. Because of the short food supply, trout usually run small but are willing biters.

LOW-GRADIENT FREESTONE streams wind through bogs, meadows or woodlands. They have sand or silt bottoms, and undercut banks or deadfalls for cover. Some, fed by springs or meltwater, have clear water; others, fed by swamp drainage, have tea-colored water.

Limestone Streams

LOW-GRADIENT LIMESTONE streams have some spring flow, move slowly, and have a meandering streambed composed of silt, sand or small gravel. The depth is fairly uniform, with few riffles. In meadow streams, a common variety, overhanging grass is the primary cover for trout.

MEDIUM-GRADIENT LIMESTONE streams normally have some spring flow, moderate to fast current, a pool-riffle-run configuration, and a streambed composed of gravel, rubble or boulders. Many such streams flow over exposed limestone bedrock and have large numbers of crayfish.

Other Common Stream Types

TAILWATER STREAMS, fed by cold water from the depths of a reservoir, produce trophy trout. The stream level may fluctuate greatly during the day as water is released to drive power turbines. This limits insect populations, but baitfish and crustaceans are plentiful.

SPRING CREEKS, either limestone or freestone, arise from groundwater sources. They have slow to moderate current, very clear water, lush weed growth, and heavy insect populations. Some produce tremendous numbers of crustaceans and surprisingly large trout.

Run — Deeper than a riffle, with moderate to fast current; surface not as turbulent; bottom materials range from small gravel to rubble.

Riffle — Shallow water; fast current; turbulent surface; gravel, rubble or boulder bottom. In big rivers, these areas are called *rapids*.

FAST WATER in a riffle excavates a deeper channel, or run, immediately downstream. As current digs the run

Understanding Moving Water

Why does a trout lie upstream of a boulder when there is a noticeable eddy on the downstream side? Why does it choose a feeding station on bottom when most of its food is drifting on the surface? And why does a fly cast near the bank drift more slowly than the fly line in midstream?

Questions like these have a direct bearing on your ability to find and catch trout. Answering them correctly requires a basic understanding of stream hydraulics. The trout lies on the upstream side of the boulder because an eddy forms upstream of an object as well as downstream. The trout chooses a feeding station on bottom because friction with bottom

deeper, the velocity slows, forming a pool. Because of the slower current, sediment is deposited at the pool's

materials slows the current to as little as one-fourth the speed of the surface current. Similarly, the fly next to the bank drifts more slowly than the fly line because friction with the bank slows the current (diagrams at right).

Understanding how moving water shapes the stream channel and learning to recognize the resulting habitat types can also improve your chances of finding trout. In most good trout streams, the current creates a riffle-run-pool sequence that repeats itself along the stream course. A deep pool may hold big brown trout, but rainbows and smaller browns are more likely to be found in runs. Riffles hold only small trout during midday, but are important morning and evening feeding areas for most species.

A normal stream tends to meander, or weave, as it flows downstream. Current flowing to the outside of a bend becomes swifter, eroding the streambed and sometimes carving an undercut bank. At the same time, current on the opposite side of the stream slackens, causing silt to settle out and fill in the streambed. In almost all cases, the outside bends hold the most trout.

Most stream fishermen know that water plunging over a falls digs out a pool at the base. But many do not realize that the turbulence caused by the plunging water undercuts the base of the falls, forming a cave that makes one of the best feeding and resting stations in the stream (diagram at far right).

Pool — Deep, slow-moving water with a flat surface; bottom of silt, sand or small gravel. Similar but shallower areas are called *flats*.

downstream end, raising the streambed and channeling the water into a smaller area. Because the flow is more constricted, the current speeds up, forming another riffle. The sequence then repeats.

Basic Stream Hydraulics

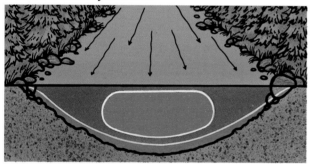

CURRENT SPEED varies within the stream cross-section. The blue area has slow current; the purple, moderate current; the red, fast current. Water in the fast zone moves up to four times as fast as that in the slow zone.

EDDIES form both upstream and downstream of an obstacle such as a boulder. Many anglers do not realize that there is an eddy on the upstream side; they work only the downstream eddy, bypassing a lot of trout.

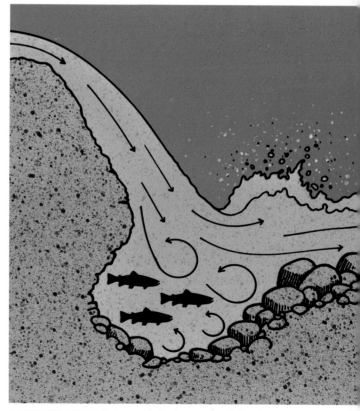

PLUNGE POOLS form at the base of a falls as a result of the cascading water. Plunge-pool depth usually exceeds the distance from the crest of the falls to the water level. A dugout often forms at the base of the falls.

39

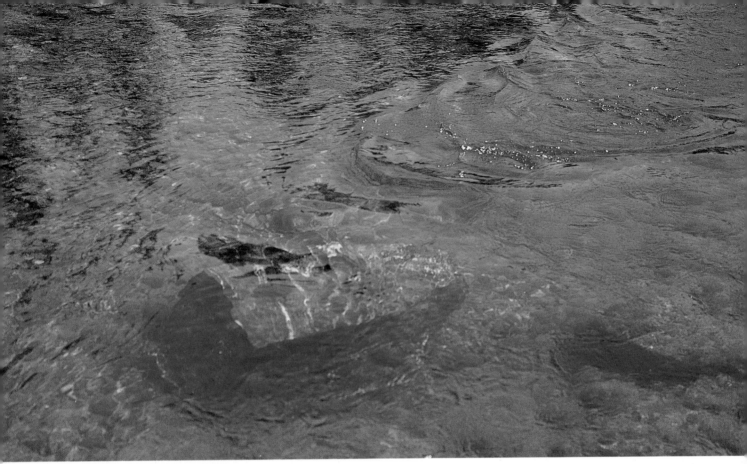

BOILS form when current deflects upward off an under-water obstruction, usually a boulder. When you see a boil, there is a good chance that trout are holding in the eddy just downstream of the obstruction. But the boil forms farther downstream, so you must cast well up-stream of the boil to catch the trout.

Reading the Water

An experienced stream fisherman can learn a great deal about a stream simply by walking its banks and "reading" the water. He observes current patterns, surface disturbances, coloration differences, changes in bottom type, and other clues that reveal trout and salmon hiding spots.

Current patterns pinpoint the location of rocks, logs or other underwater objects that shelter the fish from the moving water. Current pushing against a bank may indicate an undercut that offers cover. The seam between fast and slow current makes a good feeding station; trout hold in the slower water waiting for food to drift by in the faster water.

Novice stream fishermen pass up any water where the surface is broken and ripply, mistakenly assum-ing it is too fast and shallow for trout. But if you look carefully, this water may have slack-water poc-kets. A small pocket behind a rock might be home to a good-sized trout, even though the water is less than a foot deep.

Bottom makeup also dictates where trout will be found. A section of stream with a sandy bottom gen-erally supports fewer trout than a section with a rocky or gravelly bottom. Important trout foods, especially larval aquatic insects, thrive among rocks and gravel, but may be completely absent in sand.

If possible, examine the stream from a high angle to get an idea of streambed contour and location of boulders, submerged logs, weed patches and other underwater objects. You can see most on a bright day when the sun is at its highest. Polarized sunglasses will remove the glare so you can see into the water.

Many trout streams have been damaged by erosion, beaver activity, channelization or logging. Natural-resources agencies and sportsmen's clubs some-times reclaim these streams by installing devices to deepen the channel and provide good cover for trout.

Stream-improvement structures may be difficult to see because fisheries managers take great pains to make them look natural. The trick to fishing a re-claimed stream is simply learning to recognize the various structures and understanding how they work. Then you can use the fishing techniques that would work in similar natural cover. The most com-mon stream-improvement devices are shown at right.

Tips on Reading the Water

UNDERCUT BANKS can be found by watching the current. If it is angling toward a bank, rather than flowing parallel to it, the bank is undercut.

DEEP HOLES appear as dark areas in the streambed. Trout move into holes to escape the current. The best holes have boulders or logs for cover.

WEED PATCHES may be difficult to see, especially in low light. But the weeds usually slow the current, creating slack spots on the surface.

CURRENT SEAMS are easy to spot because debris and foam usually collect in the slack water, near the edge of the fast water.

CHECK your favorite stream at low-water stage to find deep holes and objects like submerged logs that could hold trout when the water is higher.

Common Stream-Improvement Devices

CRIB SHELTERS, manmade undercut banks supported by pilings are built along outside bends. Water is deflected toward them by a rock or log structure on the opposite bank, scouring the bank under the crib. The left photo shows the shelter under construction, the right photo a year later.

HEWITT RAMPS, used mainly on high-gradient streams, function much like small dams. A deeper pool forms above; a scour hole below.

41

LIGHT RAIN or moderate wind disturbs the surface enough that trout cannot see you clearly. The fish feed heavily on terrestrial foods washed in by the rain or wind and are not nearly as spooky as they are when the surface is calm. But heavy rain pelting the surface or intense wind puts the trout down.

Good Conditions for Trout Fishing

SLIGHTLY MURKY water allows trout to see the lure, but makes it difficult for them to see you. The clarity is best when the stream is rising or after it starts to fall.

OVERCAST skies eliminate harsh shadows that can spook trout. The fish do not hesitate to leave cover to search for food, sometimes moving into riffles in midday.

Weather

In stream fishing for trout and salmon, nothing is more important than weather. It affects the clarity, temperature and water level of the stream, which largely determine where the fish will be found and how well they will bite.

The most important factor is rain. Trout often start to feed when the sky darkens before a storm. A light to moderate rain slightly clouds the water, washes terrestrial foods into the stream, and increases the flow, causing more immature aquatic insects to drift downstream. These changes make for ideal feeding conditions and good fishing. A heavy rain, on the other hand, seems to turn the fish off. If the downpour is prolonged, it muddies the water so much that the fish cannot see, and with the rising water, they abandon their normal locations.

Rain has even more effect on anadromous trout and salmon. Fish entering a stream to spawn tend to stage up at the stream mouth. A few will enter the stream at normal flow, but the majority wait for the increased flow resulting from a heavy rain. Fishing is poor as long as the stream stays muddy, but improves rapidly when the water starts to clear.

Air temperature also has a dramatic effect on feeding activity. Most trout and salmon species feed heaviest at water temperatures from 55° to 60° F. On a typical stream, warm, sunny weather early or late in the season will drive the water temperature to that range by midafternoon, triggering an insect hatch and starting a feeding spree. But in summer, the same type of weather warms the water too much by midafternoon, so fishing is poor. Trout bite better in the morning or evening, when the water is cooler.

Another important element is cloud cover. In sunny weather, trout are extra-wary, seeking the cover of boulders, logs or undercut banks. But in cloudy weather, they are more aggressive and more willing to leave cover to find food. Anadromous fish tend to migrate more under cloudy skies.

Windy weather also makes trout more aggressive. The wind blows insects into the stream and trout start feeding. But trout have difficulty spotting small insects when the surface is choppy, so dry-fly fishing is not as effective as it would be if the water were calm.

Poor Conditions for Trout Fishing

HIGH, MUDDY WATER makes it impossible for trout to see your bait. Fly fishing is usually a waste of time, but natural-bait fishermen still catch a few trout.

SUNNY, CALM weather makes trout extra-wary. They are quick to notice shadows from your body, your rod and even your fly line. They hold tight to cover until evening.

Equipment

Fly Line

A well-stocked tackle shop offers a bewildering assortment of fly lines. They come in different weights, different tapers and a selection of colors. Some float, some sink, and some do a little of each. But choosing the right lines for various situations need not be difficult. Your decision depends mainly on the size of your fly, how far you want to cast it, and how deep you want it to sink. Other factors that may influence your selection include the wariness of the trout, whether the surface is smooth or broken, and the amount of wind.

Most fly lines are 80 to 100 feet long, consisting of a core of braided nylon or Dacron with a plastic coating. The plastic may be impregnated with air bubbles or lead powder to make it float or sink, and it may vary in thickness so the line tapers. When selecting and using fly lines, consider the following:

LINE WEIGHT. Your fly line must be heavy enough to propel the fly you are casting. But the heavier it is, the more it will disturb the surface when it lands. Delicacy is most important in calm water or when trout seem especially spooky; it matters less when the surface is broken or trout are gorging themselves

during a heavy hatch. As a general rule, the heavier the line, the farther you can cast and the easier it is to drive your fly into the wind.

Fly-line weight is designated by numbers that represent the weight of the front 30 feet of the line. Practically all trout and salmon fishing is done with line weights 2 to 12.

Light-weight lines (2 to 4) give you the most delicate presentation. With line this light, you can cast small, unweighted flies, but you cannot cast as far, and casting in a strong wind may be difficult.

Medium-weight lines (5 to 7) are the most versatile. They can handle flies of almost any size and perform well in most fishing situations.

Heavy-weight lines (8 and 9) can deliver large flies and punch through the wind. Shooting-head lines are most often used in weights of 8 or heavier.

Extra-heavy lines (10 to 12) are used mainly for steelhead and salmon. Most lead-core shooting heads do not carry standard weight designations, but usually are cast with 10-weight rods. Eleven- and twelve-weight lines are less popular in North America than in Europe, where anglers use them with two-handed salmon rods.

LINE TAPER. A fly line that tapers, or varies in diameter along its length, casts more efficiently than a level line. The forward section, or *front taper*, is thin at the tip but expands to a thicker section called the *belly*. The length and position of the belly determine how far and how delicately a given line will cast. The tapers used most in trout and salmon fishing are:

Running Line   Belly   Tip

Weight-Forward (WF) — The belly is short and near the forward end, so it shoots out easily, pulling the thinner *running line* with it. Weight-forward lines are the best choice for beginners. They are good for distance casting, but do not roll-cast well.

Tip   Belly   Tip

Double-Taper (DT) — The belly is long and in the middle of the line; both ends taper equally. A double-taper line does not cast as far as a weight-forward, but is easier to *mend* (p. 77) and more economical; you can reverse it when one end wears out.

Mono Running Line   Head   Tip

Shooting Head or Shooting Taper (ST) — This special-purpose line consists of about 30 feet of level or tapered fly line, loop-spliced to 100 feet of 15- to 30-pound mono running line. The mono is usually flattened or oval-shaped to minimize coiling. The heavy head easily pulls the mono, so you can cast extreme distances. But shooting heads have some drawbacks. They lack delicacy, and the long running line tangles easily. To minimize tangling, use a shooting basket or substitute a special thin fly line for the mono. But the fly line reduces casting distance.

Some fly casters carry several shooting heads, both floating and sinking, then connect them to the running line as needed. This eliminates the need to change the entire line for a different type of fishing.

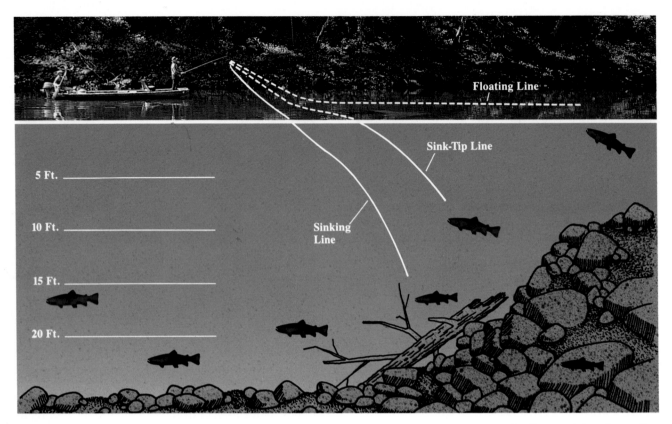

LINE FLOTATION. Floating lines (designated by the letter F) are the obvious choice for fishing dry flies. Because the line floats high on the surface film, little effort is required to pick it up for another cast or to mend it. Floating lines can also be used with sinking flies, with or without added weight such as split-shot or lead leader-wrap. With a floating line and a long leader, you can fish a sinking fly several feet down.

Sinking lines (S) come in different densities, ranging from slow-sinking to extremely fast-sinking, for different depths, current speeds and retrieve speeds. Because they sink over their entire length, they are difficult to control in current, and you must retrieve most of the line in order to make another cast. As a general rule, use a sinking line whenever you are fishing deeper than 10 feet.

Sink-tip lines, also called floating/sinking lines (F/S), have 5 to 20 feet of sinking line attached to a floating line. Generally, the sinking portion is a different color. The sink rate of the tip ranges from intermediate to extremely fast. Because only the tip sinks, these lines are easier than sinking lines to pick up from the water. They work well at depths of 2 to 10 feet.

LINE DESIGNATIONS. When you purchase a fly line, look for a three-part code on the label that designates the taper, weight and flotation of the line. The code WF-6-F, for instance, designates a weight-forward, 6-weight, floating fly line.

MATCHING ROD TO LINE. The weight of your line determines the power of the rod needed to handle it. If you try to cast a light line with a heavy rod, the rod will not flex enough to load (p. 70). If you try to cast a heavy line with a light rod, the rod will flex too much to propel it. Most rods, however, will handle a line one weight either side of the recommended weight.

Unfortunately, there is no standard way to measure rod power, so considerable variation exists among manufacturers. A 7-weight rod from one manufacturer may have the same power as a 5-weight rod from another. A good fly-fishing shop can help you sort out these differences.

Another complication: line weight is measured by the weight of only the front 30 feet; no consideration is given to the rest of the line. The middle portion of a double-taper line, for instance, is thicker and heavier than the same portion of a weight-forward line. So, you should select a double-taper one size lighter than a weight-forward for the same rod.

LINE COLOR. The color of a fly line is more important to the fisherman than the fish. Most fly casters prefer floating lines in bright colors because they are easiest to see and control. Sinking lines, however, usually come in various shades of brown, green or gray. In most types of fly fishing, the leader is long enough that the fish do not notice the color of the line.

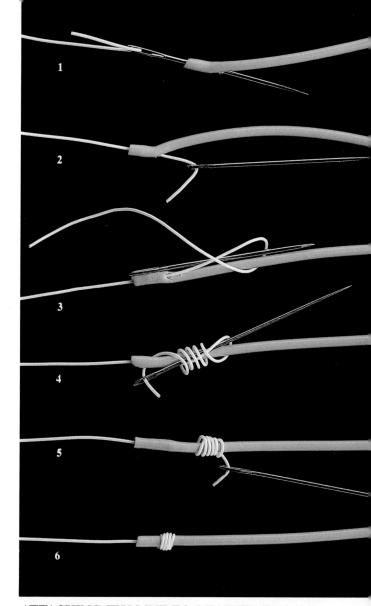

BACKING. To keep a big fish from running out all your line, always use backing under your fly line. Backing also keeps your spool full so you can reel up line more quickly, and it minimizes coiling. Most trout fishermen use 20-pound braided Dacron.

To insure that you have the right amount of backing on your reel, wind the fly line and backing on in reverse. Spool on the fly line, splice the back end of the line to the backing, and spool on enough backing to fill the reel within ⅛ to ¼ inch of the reel pillars. Then, if you have a spare spool, wind the line onto it. If not, strip the line off the spool and spread it across your yard. Then reverse ends and wind it back onto the same spool.

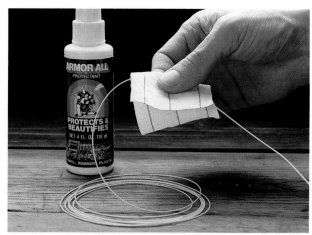

LINE CARE. If your line gets dirty or oily, simply wash it with mild soap. Floating lines need more care; use a commercial line cleaner or a protectant such as Armor All® to condition them. The line will stay pliable, float better and shoot through the guides easier. Store your line where it will not be exposed to sunlight. Practice casting on grass or water; pavement will scuff your line. Gasoline and insect repellent can also damage the line's surface.

ATTACHING FLY LINE TO LEADER. The most common knot for this purpose is the nail knot. But the needle knot (shown above) offers some advantages, mainly that the leader comes out the center of the fly line, so the knot slides easily through the rod guides.

To tie a needle knot, (1) run a needle into the fly line, and out again about ½ inch up the line. Thread the mono through the eye of the needle. (2) Pull the needle through the line. (3) Lay the needle along the line and begin making wraps around them. (4) Complete five wraps, snug but not tight, then thread the mono through the eye. (5) Pull the needle out, making sure the mono wraps lie smooth, without crossing. (6) Tighten and trim.

Instead of tying the leader directly to the line, you can join them with a mono connector (p. 68). This way, you can change leaders quickly. The mono connector is attached to the line with a needle knot.

The needle knot also works well for connecting the fly line to the backing.

49

Fly Leaders

The importance of selecting the right fly leader cannot be overstated. The proper leader enables you to fish your fly naturally, so it doesn't spook the trout. It also transmits the energy of the cast, rolling over smoothly and delivering the fly on target.

The main considerations in selecting a leader are taper, length, and tippet size:

TAPER. Like a fly line, a leader must be tapered for best casting performance. Otherwise, the energy of the cast may be lost before it reaches the fly, and the cast ends with the fly atop a coiled leader.

Fly leaders consist of a gradually tapering butt (about 60 percent of leader length), a rapidly tapering transition section (about 20 percent of length), and a level tip section or *tippet* (about 20 percent of length).

Modern tapered leaders come in two styles: knotted and knotless. A knotted leader normally has three to eight sections of monofilament of different diameters, tied together with blood knots (p. 68). To insure that the energy of the cast is transferred smoothly from line to leader, the thickest part of the leader butt should measure .017 inches for 2- to 4-weight fly line, .019 inches for 5- to 7-weight line, and .021 inches for line weights of 8 or over. For good knot strength, adjacent sections should differ in diameter by no more than .002 inches.

A knotted leader can be modified to suit your needs, and worn sections can be cut out and new ones tied in. But the knots weaken the leader and may pick up bits of weeds or debris.

Knotless leaders are stronger and do not catch debris. But they are more expensive, and if they do not have the right taper to turn over smoothly, there is nothing you can do.

How to Make a Knotted Leader

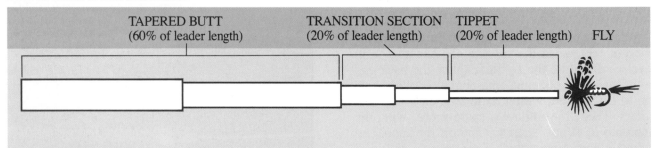

TAPERED BUTT (60% of leader length)   TRANSITION SECTION (20% of leader length)   TIPPET (20% of leader length)   FLY

Tips for Using Leaders

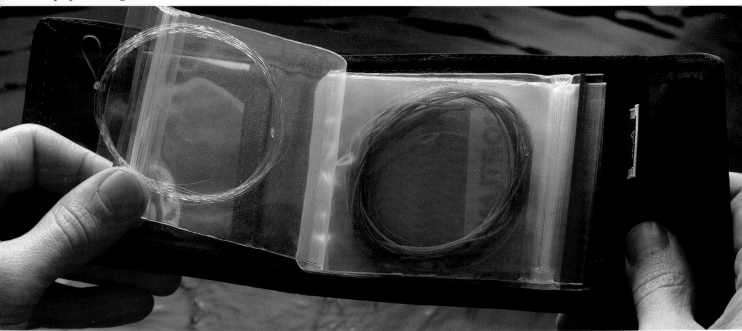

LEADER WALLETS are handy for storing leaders with different lengths and tippet sizes. Coil the leader around your hand before placing it in a vinyl pocket. If desired, label each pocket with a waterproof marker.

With any leader, the tippet becomes shorter as new flies are tied on and worn sections are cut off. Rather than replacing the whole leader when the tippet becomes too short, simply replace the tippet. You can buy tippet material in 25-yard spools.

LENGTH. The length of your leader depends on the type of fly. A sinking fly fished with a sinking or sink-tip line requires a short leader, from 3 to 4 feet. Strikes on sinking flies may be difficult to detect, and a short leader gives you a more direct connection. Also, a short leader pulls the fly deeper. A dry or sinking fly fished with a floating line requires a long leader, from 7½ to 12 feet.

With dry flies, the long leader can be manipulated to alight in a series of S-curves. This way, the fly floats freely for a longer time before *drag* (p. 75) sets in. A long tippet is especially important to insure a drag-free drift.

TIPPET DIAMETER. The proper tippet diameter depends on the size of your fly. Always use the lightest tippet that will cast the fly efficiently. A light tippet allows the fly to drift more freely, but if it is too light, it will not support the fly and will collapse in a heap at the end of the cast.

Tippet diameter is rated in "X" numbers; the higher the number, the smaller the diameter. As a rule of thumb, divide the fly size by 3 to determine the proper tippet diameter. The chart at right provides some general guidelines.

Leader length and tippet diameter also depend on the size of the stream, clarity of the water, and wind conditions, as well as the size and wariness of the fish. On a very small stream or in windy weather, you may need a shorter-than-normal leader. On a very clear stream or when trout are extra-wary, your leader should be longer than normal. A heavy tippet improves your chances of landing a big trout, but reduces your odds of getting the fish to strike in the first place.

LEADER CARE. Mono leaders require little care, but you should store them in a lightproof package and check their strength and pliability before using. Heat, sunlight or fluorescent light can weaken the leader and make it brittle. Check your leader often for nicks and abrasion.

TIPPET SIZE (inches)	DIAMETER	FLY SIZE	POUND TEST*
0X	.011	2-⅛	6.5-15.5
1X	.010	2-6	5.5-13.5
2X	.009	4-8	4.5-11.5
3X	.008	8-12	3.8-8.5
4X	.007	10-14	3.1-5.5
5X	.006	12-16	2.4-4.5
6X	.005	16-20	1.4-3.5
7X	.004	20-24	1.1-2.5
8X	.003	24-28	0.75-1.75

*tippets of the same diameter vary in strength depending on the brand of monofilament

SELECT hard monofilament for the butt of a knotted leader. Hard mono is stiff, so the leader will unroll straighter on a cast. Do not use hard mono for tippets; it's weaker than soft mono and the stiffness will hinder fly action.

USE a braided-butt leader when fishing with a light tippet. The braid stretches easily, so you won't snap the tippet on the hook set. Follow the manufacturer's instructions to attach your fly line to the hollow butt.

Fly Rods & Reels

RODS. In spinning and baitcasting, it's important to select the right rod, but the selection is not as critical as in fly fishing. A fly rod propels the line, which in turn propels the fly; if the rod is not matched to the line, casting is next to impossible. When choosing a fly rod, consider the following:

Material. In the late 1940s, fiberglass rods revolutionized fly fishing. They were considerably cheaper than the old bamboo rods, yet lighter and stiffer, so they could handle a fly line more easily. With the introduction of graphite in 1972, rod-building technology took another quantum leap.

Today's graphite rods weigh 20 to 25 percent less than glass rods of the same stiffness, and 40 to 45 percent less than bamboo. Consequently, graphite rods can be longer and lighter, yet more powerful. And you can cast farther with less effort.

Because of the obvious advantages of graphite, fewer and fewer glass rods are being produced. For those who enjoy the romance of fishing with a bamboo rod, a few manufacturers and custom rodmakers still build them. Some old bamboo rods have become collector's items, commanding prices of several thousand dollars.

Power. For peak casting performance, the power or stiffness of your fly rod should match the weight of your fly line. If the rod is too light, it will flex too much and lose its casting power. Too heavy, and it will not flex enough to propel the line.

Most fly rods have a line-weight printed near the grip. As a rule, you can use line one size lighter or heavier than the recommended weight.

Rod Action. The word "action" may be the most misused term among fishermen. Some confuse action with power; others say "this rod has a nice action," meaning that it feels good in the hand.

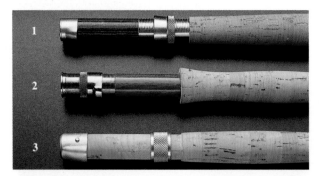

REEL SEATS include (1) down-locking, used on light rods; (2) up-locking, used on heavier rods to prevent unscrewing, and for more length behind the reel so the spool won't rub clothing; (3) sliding-band, to reduce weight on bamboo rods and light graphite rods.

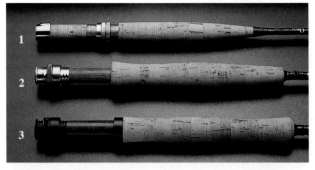

GRIPS include (1) cigar, for short- to medium-range casting with light rods; (2) half Wells, with a thicker front for more casting leverage and a raised middle for a better grip; (3) full Wells, with raised front for even more casting leverage, and a raised middle.

In reality, "action" refers to the way the rod flexes, which is determined by the taper. Slow-action rods taper slowly from butt to tip and flex over their entire length. Fast-action rods taper quickly and flex most near the tip. Medium-action rods have an intermediate taper and flexing point.

A faster rod forms a narrower loop which travels more rapidly and has less air resistance, resulting in greater distance and accuracy. Faster rods also "dampen" more quickly after the cast, so the tip doesn't bounce and throw waves into the line. The waves increase air resistance, reduce distance and cause a sloppy delivery.

A slower rod absorbs more shock, a big advantage when fishing dry flies with light tippets. And a slower rod makes it easier to control casting distance. Because the loop is not as narrow, the line speed is slower, so you can easily stop the line when the fly is over the target. But the wide loop reduces casting distance considerably.

Unfortunately, there are no industry standards to designate action, and some rod makers don't even try. One manufacturer's "slow" rod may have the same action as another's "medium" rod. But an experienced tackle-shop employee can help you make your decision.

Length. A 7½- to 9-foot fly rod suits most trout-fishing situations, but longer and shorter rods also have their uses.

In the past, fishermen shied away from longer rods because they were too heavy. But today's graphite rods are so light that greater lengths are becoming popular. Long rods give you more casting power, make it easier to mend the line (p. 77), and help you keep your backcast high enough to avoid streamside brush. Also, with the rod tip high it's easier to control your line and fly on the drift. Steelhead and salmon anglers use rods up to 10½ feet for making long casts and handling these powerful fish.

Short rods cast narrower loops and are easier to handle on narrow, brushy streams. They also make it easier to place a fly beneath an overhang, and to land trout in tight spots. Anglers on brush-lined creeks sometimes use fly rods as short as 6 feet.

REELS. Choosing a fly reel is not nearly as complicated as choosing the right fly rod or line. The reel serves only to store the line, and to provide tension when a fish makes a long run. When selecting a fly reel, consider the following:

Reel Action. The action of a reel is the way it retrieves line. With a single-action reel, the spool turns once for each turn of the handle; with a multiplying reel, it turns more than once.

A FLY REEL will accommodate a range of about three line weights. The smaller reel (foreground) is designed for 2- to 4-weight lines, plus backing; the larger, 9- to 11-weight.

Single-action reels are adequate for most trout fishing. Multiplying reels, though heavier, are better for powerful fish like steelhead. They allow you to take up slack in a hurry should a fish run toward you. Both actions are highly reliable.

Both types of reels are available in direct-drive and anti-reverse models. Direct drives are more common; the handle turns when the spool does, so if a big fish takes line, the handle turns backward. Should you accidently touch the whirling handle, your tippet would snap. On anti-reverse models, the handle does not turn backward with the spool.

Drag. When a big trout grabs your fly and rockets away, you'll need a good drag to prevent spool overrun and tire the fish. Ratchet-type drags, which emit an audible click, are simplest and most popular; disk drags, which are silent, are smoother and provide more tension. Both are adjusted with a knob on the side of the reel. Many reels have exposed spool rims: you can add more tension when a fish runs by pressing your palm on the rim.

Capacity and Weight. Check the capacity information listed in the literature that comes with the reel to be sure it can hold the line and backing. For most trout fishing, use 50 yards of backing; for steelhead and salmon, 100 yards.

A light reel is less tiring to cast with than a heavy one. As a rule, light reels are more expensive because they are machined from solid aluminum rather than stamped from sheet metal. The spool and frame fit more precisely, so there is less chance of the leader slipping between them.

Spinning
& Baitcasting Tackle

Stream-trout anglers use a variety of spinning and baitcasting tackle for fishing hardware and natural-bait rigs. Here are some guidelines for selecting rods, reels and line:

RODS. Most trout fishermen prefer rods made of graphite because they are lighter and more sensitive than similar fiberglass rods. But all graphite rods are not the same. Some have a considerably higher graphite content, and there are different types of graphite materials. You will get noticably better performance from rods made of extra-stiff, or *high-modulus*, graphite. The rods most commonly used in stream-trout fishing include:

Light Spinning — In small streams, fishermen commonly use light to ultralight spinning rods with 2- to 6-pound mono. Most rods for this type of fishing measure 4½ to 5½ feet in length, have a medium action, and are designed for lures from ⅓₂ to ⅜ ounce. A medium-action rod flexes enough to cast most light lures and baits, yet has enough backbone for a good hook-set. To cast extremely light lures, you need a slow-action rod.

Medium Spinning — These work best in medium to large streams with good-sized trout. They will easily handle ¼- to ⅝-ounce lures, which are needed for adequate casting distance and getting to bottom. A typical outfit for this situation includes a 6- to 7-foot medium-action rod and 6- to 8-pound mono.

Steelhead and Salmon — A long, stiff rod, combined with a high-capacity reel, is ideal for casting long distances. This type of rod also gives you more control of the line, better sensitivity and more power for tiring the fish.

Some rod manufacturers now produce a line of steelhead and salmon rods that includes both spinning and baitcasting models. Most of these rods measure 8 to 10 feet in length. They will handle lures

LIGHT SPINNING GEAR works well on small streams where brush or trees restrict your casting motion. A sidearm or backhand casting stroke places your lure beneath the branches.

MEDIUM SPINNING GEAR is the best choice for wider, deeper or faster-moving streams. Here, heavier lures are often necessary to make long casts and to reach bottom in the swift current.

from ½ to 2 ounces and mono from 10- to 20-pound test. For drift fishing (p. 104), steelhead and salmon fishermen often match an 8- to 9-foot fly rod with a spinning reel.

REELS. Make sure your spinning reel has a large-diameter spool and a smooth drag. On many spinning reels, the spool is so small that even limp mono tends to coil. For a light or ultralight rod, spool diameter should be at least 1½ inches; for a medium-power rod, 1¾ inches; for a steelhead rod, 2 inches.

A smooth drag is important in any stream fishing; if your drag sticks, even a small trout can snap your line in fast current. As a rule, front drags are smoother than rear drags. If possible, test the drag by attaching a 6- to 8-ounce weight to the line, lifting the weight off the ground, then gradually loosening the drag. The weight should drop slowly and evenly; if it drops in jerks, look for another reel.

The drag is equally important on a baitcasting reel. Cheap reels often have "all-or-nothing" drags. When set light, the drag slips so much you can't set the hook. If you tighten it, it grabs too much and a big fish will break your line.

LINE. Trout are extremely line-shy, so most anglers use clear mono, or mono shaded to match the water color. Fluorescent line or other high-visibility line is not recommended. Hard-finish lines are popular for drift fishing because they can take more abrasion, but they're too stiff for most trout fishing. Limp mono works better for casting light lures and baits; it has less *memory*, meaning it is not as likely to form coils that reduce casting distance. But limp mono nicks easier, so you must retie hooks and lures more often.

SALMON AND STEELHEAD GEAR (photo at right) is needed to handle large salmonids in big rivers. The long, stiff rod gives you extra casting distance and more leverage for turning a powerful fish.

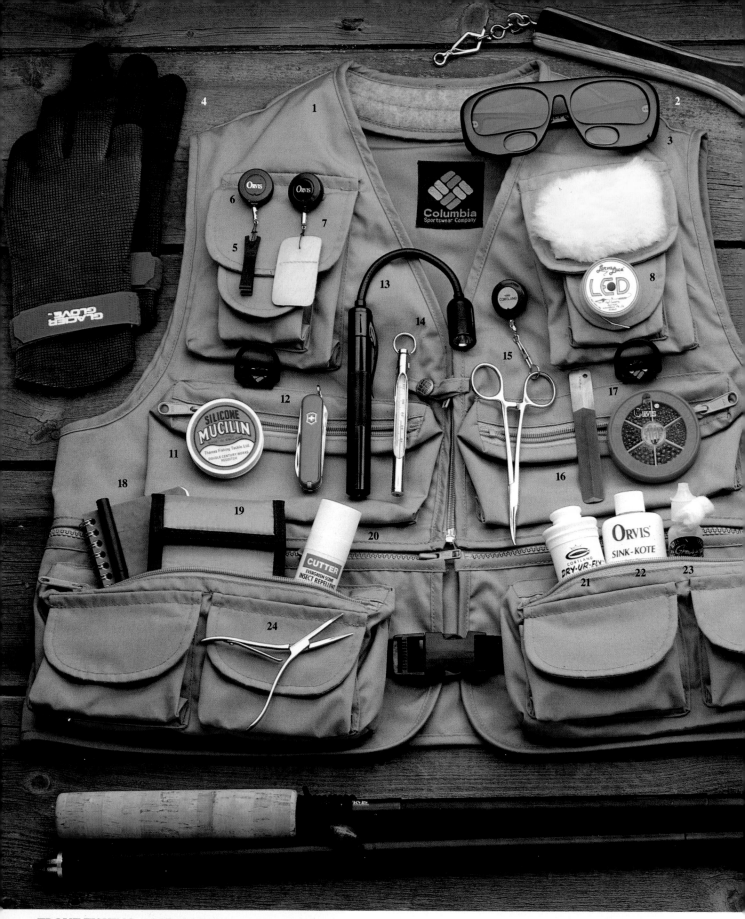

TROUT-FISHING ACCESSORIES include: (1) fishing vest, (2) landing net with French snap, (3) polarized sunglasses, (4) neoprene gloves, (5) line clipper on (6) retractor reel, (7) leader straightener on retractor, (8) leader wrap, (9) fly box with spring-loaded lids, (10) large, foam-lined fly box, (11) floatant, (12) Swiss Army knife, (13) gooseneck light, (14) water thermometer, (15) forceps on retractor, (16) hook file, (17) split-shot assort-

Trout-Fishing Accessories

ment, (18) notebook and pen, (19) leader wallet, (20) insect repellent, (21) silicone fly desiccant, (22) leader sink, (23) fly line cleaner, (24) needlenose pliers, (25) tippet material, (26) wading staff.

When you're wading a trout stream, you may walk a mile or more from your starting point. Should you forget something, it's a long walk back to your car. To avoid such problems, wear a fishing vest with lots of pockets and carry your accessories with you. You probably won't need all the accessories described below, but this list may give you some ideas:

Vest - Should have enough pockets to carry the gear you normally need for a day's fishing, including raingear. Look for a vest with zippers on the large pockets, Velcro fasteners on the small ones, and a ring or loop at the rear of the collar for attaching a landing net. Make sure the vest is large enough that you can wear a heavy sweater underneath. Short vests are available for wading in deep water, and vests with mesh backs and shoulders for hot weather.

Landing Net - Choose one with a short handle and cotton mesh. Cotton is softer and less abrasive than synthetic material, so it's the best choice for catch-and-release fishing. Attach the net to your vest with a French clip, so you can detach it quickly.

Fly Box - Fly fishermen often carry several fly boxes. Dry flies should be stored in a box with large compartments to avoid crushing the delicate hackle. A simple plastic box with a tight-fitting lid and good-sized compartments will do, but a box that has compartments with individual spring-loaded lids protects your flies better from wind and rain.

With other flies, the type of box is less critical. Some boxes have metal clips to hold the flies, but the clips are usually too large to hold flies smaller than size 14. Some boxes are magnetic, and in others the flies are embedded in foam; the foam boxes are best for tiny flies. Traditional fleece-lined fly books are still used, but if a fly is stored wet, the fleece absorbs moisture, and the hook rusts.

Needlenose Pliers — Used for removing hooks from large trout and for flattening barbs in catch-and-release fishing. Select a small, lightweight model, preferably made of stainless steel.

Forceps — Best for removing hooks from smaller trout.

Clippers — Ordinary fingernail clippers will work for cutting line, but specially designed clippers are much better. They stay sharper longer, and have a small pin for cleaning head cement out of the eyes of fly hooks.

Retractor Reel — This small reel has a retractable cord for attaching clippers, forceps or other commonly used accessories. The reel pins to your vest.

Priest — For quickly killing trout you wish to keep.

Split-Shot — An assortment of split-shot in small sizes is needed to take sinking flies deep. A fly with split-shot 6 to 12 inches ahead of it swims more naturally than one with lead wire on the hook shank. Split-shot are also used for drifting live bait.

Leader Wrap — The flat lead wire can be wrapped on your leader as a substitute for split-shot.

Floatant — Silicone floatants in paste, liquid or spray form will keep a dry fly floating longer.

Silicone Powder — This drying agent quickly removes water or fish slime from a dry fly and reshapes the hackle. Place your fly in the container and shake; the powder will absorb the water.

Leader Sink — Apply to leader so it sinks quickly when using wet flies or nymphs.

Leader Straightener — The most popular type is a piece of leather lined with silicone-treated rubber. Squeeze your tippet in the rubber and pull it through to remove any kinks or curls.

Line Cleaner — For removing dirt and oil from your fly line.

Water Thermometer — Select a fast-registering thermometer, preferably one with a metal tube. Tie the tube to a cord long enough to reach bottom.

Insect Net — Used to scoop insects from the water for identification. A small aquarium net will do. Some anglers carry small bottles so they can take the insects home for study.

Polarized Glasses — Used to reduce glare so you can see bottom features and fish. Glass lenses resist scratching better than plastic. Prescription polarized lenses are available at most eyewear stores. You can also get glasses with small magnifying lenses for examining small objects.

Insect Repellent — Stick repellent is best. Avoid lotion types that adhere to your hands; they could damage your fly line.

Tippet Material — Carry tippet spools in all the diameters you normally use to rebuild leaders.

Leader Wallet — Used for storing extra leaders. Choose a wallet with zip-lock plastic holders.

Notebook — Used to record information on insect hatches and other streamside observations that could be useful in future years.

Vest Light — For changing flies, unhooking fish and finding your way in the dark. Select one with a clip that attaches to your vest, and with a gooseneck for directing the light.

Stomach Pump — Used for extracting stomach contents from trout you wish to release. The pump is simply a plastic tube with a rubber squeeze-bulb at one end.

Creel — Canvas or wicker creels are best; when you wet them, evaporation keeps the fish cool.

Tape Measure — For personal records, many fishermen like to measure their trout before releasing them. Where length regulations apply, you may need to measure a trout to determine if it is legal size. A small tape measure will do, but you can also buy adhesive-backed tapes that stick to the butt section of your fly rod.

Hook Hone — Fly hooks are easily damaged by bumping rocks. The point can be resharpened with a small jewelry file or stone.

Wading Staff — Used for keeping your balance in fast current. Collapsible staffs made of aluminum tubing are easy to carry in your vest, but wooden staffs are also popular.

Swiss Army Knife — The knife blade can be used for gutting trout, the scissors for trimming hackle, the screwdriver for fixing a reel, the tweezers for examining insects, the toothpick for tying a nail knot.

Rain Jacket — Keep a light rain parka in the large pocket on the back of your vest.

Fingerless Gloves — These keep your hands warm and dry, yet allow you to tie knots. The warmest ones are made of neoprene.

Waders and Hip Boots

Modern materials have made waders lighter, tougher, safer and more comfortable. The biggest improvement is the development of neoprene stocking-foot waders. Neoprene is warm, remarkably durable and flexible enough to mold to your body. If you fall into the water, your waders won't fill and the closed-cell foam will keep you afloat. Neoprene waders can be easily repaired with a special adhesive should they develop a leak. But they have two drawbacks: they're expensive and too warm for hot weather.

Nylon waders are better for warm-weather fishing. They come in stocking-foot or boot-foot models and are relatively inexpensive. Latex waders are more pliable than nylon. They come only in stocking-foot, and are intermediate in weight and warmth between neoprene and nylon.

Hip boots are ideal for shallow streams. Most are made of rubber with a boot foot, although nylon models are available in stocking foot. Hip boots with canvas or Cordura uppers wear better than all-rubber boots and are more puncture-resistant.

Basic Types of Waders and Hip Boots

BOOT-FOOT waders come with the boots attached. They are convenient to put on, but the ankles fit loosely and give little support. Some come with felt soles.

STOCKING-FOOT waders fit more snugly, so they have less current resistance. Separate wading shoes provide ankle support; the felt soles improve traction on slippery rocks.

HIP BOOTS should fit snugly around the ankle and lower calf (left). If the ankle portion is too large (right), the boot will pull loose from your foot when you walk in the mud.

Wading Accessories

STREAM CLEATS fit over your wading shoes or boot-foots. They give you more traction than felt soles on mossy rocks in fast current.

GRAVEL GUARDS keep sand and rocks out of boots used with stocking-foot waders. Some waders have gravel guards built in.

WADING BELTS help keep water out of your waders should you fall. Special elastic belts are available, but an old leather belt or rope will do.

MCKENZIE RIVER BOATS normally have fiberglass or wooden hulls, but some are made of aluminum. Fiberglass and wooden hulls are quieter and have a lower center of gravity, so they're more stable. A wide hull has more lift

Boats & Motors

A good-sized river may be too deep or too fast to fish by wading. A boat makes it possible to fish more effectively, and to reach water that would otherwise be inaccessible.

Trout fishermen use small aluminum rowboats, canoes, jonboats and practically anything else that floats. But in streams with lots of fast, turbulent water, these ordinary boats may not be a good choice. Jonboats, for instance, float easily through the shallow riffles, and their open design makes for comfortable fishing. But their square bow makes them difficult to maneuver on turbulent rivers; because of their low profile, they swamp more easily than boats with higher sides.

McKenzie River boats solve the problems of low sides and square bow. Their pointed, swept-up ends

offer little water resistance, so they turn with only a stroke of the oars and are easy to hold steady in the current. They draw very little water. Most are equipped with knee braces, so the fisherman at the bow can keep his balance while standing up to cast. Another advantage is the ease of sliding the boat across current (photos at right).

Normally, the boat is controlled by oars and used only for float trips. One person rows while another fishes. Proper oar length is critical for good control; a 16-foot boat, the most popular size, requires oars of about 8½ feet. But some McKenzie boats are powered by outboards up to 15 horsepower.

McKenzie boats are widely used in the West, and are becoming more popular in the East. However, their weight and the need for a trailer to haul them limits their popularity. Another limitation: the high bow and stern tend to catch the wind, making them difficult to control on open, windswept stretches.

INFLATABLE RAFTS made of modern tear-resistant synthetic fabrics are remarkably durable and puncture-resistant. Oblong rafts in 12- to 16-foot lengths are most popular. Pontoon-style rafts have solid transoms for mounting outboards up to 25 horsepower.

JET BOATS have a heavy-duty, flat-bottomed hull and are powered by a jet-drive inboard or outboard. The jet drive (inset) does not have a propeller, but operates on the same principle as a jet engine on an airplane. Jet-drive outboards range from 25 to 150 horsepower.

and is more stable and maneuverable than a narrow one.

Inflatable rafts are used on many of the same waters as McKenzie boats. They are safe, durable, light, and much more portable. The soft bottom slides quietly over shallow riffles. But rafts aren't nearly as maneuverable as McKenzie boats, nor as comfortable to fish from.

Jet boats are ideal in shallow, rocky rivers. They plane easily over riffles where a propeller would grind rocks. Once they're on plane, they can cruise over water only 6 inches deep; but if you start up in shallow water, small rocks could be sucked into the water intake and jam the impeller. Jet drives have about one-third less power and fuel efficiency than standard outboards of the same size.

How to Maneuver a McKenzie River Boat

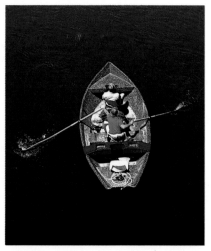

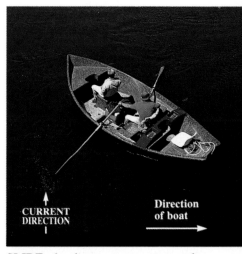

PIVOT a McKenzie River boat by pushing on one oar while pulling on the other. Because of the turned-up ends, you can easily pivot the boat while holding in place.

SLIDE the boat across current by angling the stern in the direction you want to go, then rowing upstream. It's easiest to control the boat with the stern pointed into the current.

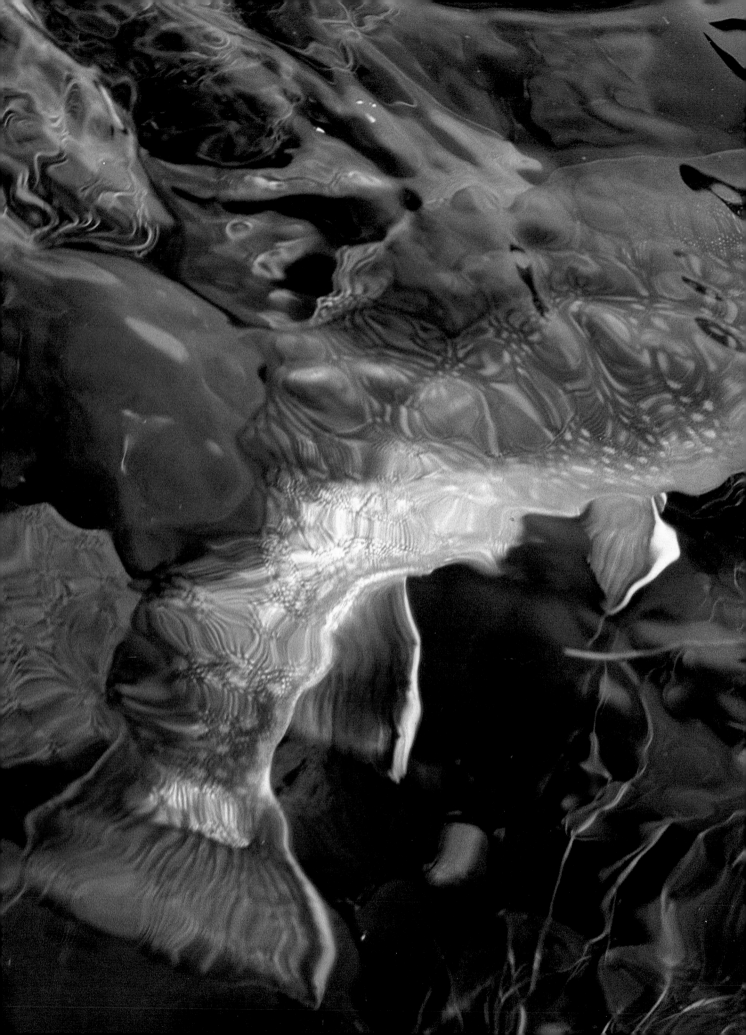

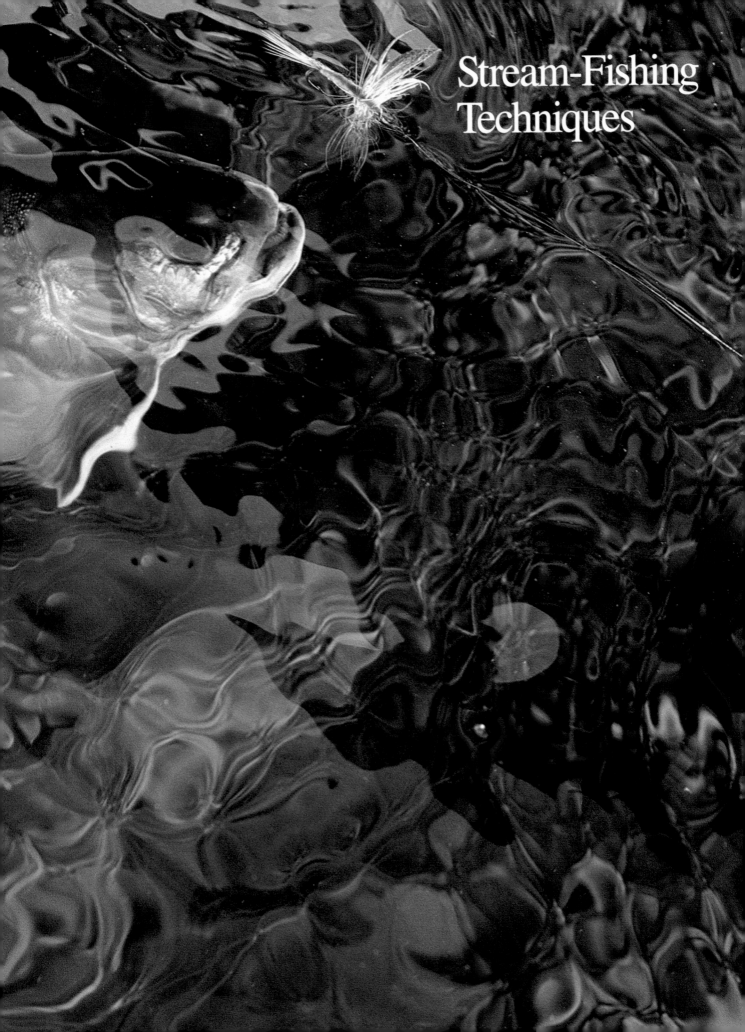

Stream-Fishing
Techniques

Stream-Fishing Basics

Trout are among the wariest of gamefish. Any quick movement or unusual sound, like the crunching of gravel or clattering of loose rocks when you wade, will send them darting for cover. But you can minimize spooking by following these guidelines:

- Keep a low profile (photo above); the lower you are, the less likely you will appear in the trout's window of vision. To fish a narrow stream, you may have to crawl to the bank and cast from a kneeling position.

- Wear drab clothing, something that blends in with the surroundings. A bright-colored shirt or cap can put the trout down in a hurry.

- In turbulent water, you can approach a trout more closely than in slow or slack water.

- Use objects such as boulders and trees to conceal your approach. If there is no place to hide, try to stay in the shadows.

- When you reach a likely spot, stand still for a few minutes before making a cast. When you first arrive, trout detect your presence and stop feeding. But after a few minutes, they may get used to you and start to feed again, even if you are plainly visible.

- Try to avoid casting over the trout's window of vision, especially with bright-colored fly line.

Wading

In small, narrow streams, you will probably want to fish from the bank to conceal yourself, but most other streams can be fished more easily by wading. When you wade, your profile is lower, your backcast is less obstructed, and you can get closer to midstream lies. To wade effectively and safely, keep these suggestions in mind:

- Don't step off the bank without first checking the depth; if possible, cross at a riffle.

- Wear felt-soled waders or stream cleats (p. 59) for traction. Rubber soles are far too slippery for wading over wet, algae-covered rocks.

- Step softly to avoid banging rocks together. Before putting your full weight on a rock, make sure it is stable so it doesn't clink against other rocks or make you lose your balance.

- Walk with short, shuffling steps to keep ripples to a minimum on quiet pools, and to better feel an uneven bottom.

- In most situations, wade upstream. Trout face into the current so you will be approaching them from behind, and not stirring up silt which will drift over them. Also, it's safer to wade upstream; if you trip, the current helps hold you up. If you wade downstream, the current may push you too fast, causing you to lose your balance.

- To move from one spot to another along a stream, walk on the bank instead of wading in the streambed and disturbing fish.

- Wear polarized glasses; they help you to spot fish and to avoid obstructions that could trip you.

Tips for Safe Wading

CARRY a wading staff to help keep your balance in fast water or on a boulder-strewn bottom. A collapsible staff can be carried in your vest.

TURN sideways when wading in fast current. This minimizes the force of the current, so your feet do not get swept out from under you.

PIVOT upstream to turn around in fast current. If you pivot downstream, the current pushes you too fast, tending to wash you off your feet.

Fly Fishing for Trout & Salmon

Why fly-fish? After all, you can catch trout and salmon by spinning or baitcasting, both of which are easier to learn.

Fly fishing is by far the oldest of these methods, with a history stretching back at least six centuries. So the modern fly angler, equipped with a lightweight graphite rod rather than a buggy-whip wooden pole, has the satisfaction of carrying on a long and colorful tradition.

But nostalgia, no matter how strong, can't account for the survival of this old-time method into the space age, or for the manifold increase in its popularity in recent years. Despite its ancient origins, fly fishing remains a versatile and productive way to outwit wary salmonids.

Many of the most common foods of trout can be imitated only with flies; even the tiniest spinning and casting lures are much too bulky. Aquatic insects, such as mayflies and caddisflies, make up most of the diet of stream trout. Imitations of these delicate creatures are much too light to be cast with ordinary spinning or baitcasting techniques.

In fact, any trout food can be imitated successfully with flies. With a 6- or 7-weight fly line and a rod to match, you can fish anything from the tiniest midge imitations, not much bigger than a gnat, on up to streamers that simulate minnows several inches long.

The most frantic angling for stream trout comes during cloudlike insect hatches. Yet it can also be the most frustrating. The fish may be rising all around you, but if you're limited to casting hardware, you're almost certainly out of luck. When rising to a hatch, trout generally refuse all imitations of other types of food.

Some of the biggest trout feed almost entirely on baitfish. In lakes, spoons and minnow plugs usually work better for these fish than streamer flies, which don't have much action in the still water. But in streams the current gives streamers an erratic, undulating movement more lifelike than the steady wobbling of hardware. And generally you can mimic the size, shape, and color of particular baitfish more closely with flies than with plugs or spoons.

Many famous trout streams have flies-only regulations. Although spinning and baitcasting equipment is sometimes allowed, such tackle makes it difficult to present a fly realistically enough for the educated trout found in these waters. For casting flies softly and maneuvering them like living creatures through a maze of currents, fly-fishing tackle nearly always works best.

Some anglers hesitate to try fly fishing because matching the hatch seems too complicated. But you don't have to know the insects by their species names, or carry scores of different fly patterns. In nearly all cases, an approximate imitation will do the job. Actually, a hatch is not so much a problem as an opportunity. Seeing exactly what the fish are feeding on is a big advantage; in most other kinds of fishing, all you can do is guess.

It's true that learning to fly-fish takes time and effort. To become really skilled may require several seasons of experience on the water. But it's also true that you can start enjoying this traditional way of angling, and start catching fish, after only a couple of brief practice sessions.

As in any other kind of fishing, the learning is part of the fun. Actually, it's a process that never ends, even if you fish a lifetime. The tips on the following pages will get you started right.

Rigging Up

When trout are rising but won't take a fly, the fisherman may wonder if he's using the wrong pattern or perhaps the wrong size. And if he hooks a fish but fails to catch it, he may ponder what mistake he made while fighting it. In both cases, however, he might be asking himself the wrong questions.

Many of the costly errors in fly fishing are made even before the first cast. To present the fly realistically and to hold a running or jumping fish, your tackle must be carefully rigged. It's tempting to rush the preliminaries, especially when you arrive at the stream and a hatch is already under way. Fly tackle takes longer to rig than other kinds of equipment, but experienced anglers know it's time well spent.

Do as much of the rigging as possible before you leave home. Tie a length of heavy monofilament to the tip of your fly line with a needle knot. For lines up to 4-weight, use .017-inch mono; for 5- to 7-weight lines, .019-inch; for 8-weight and heavier, .021-inch. In the other end of the mono, tie a perfection loop. When finished, this mono connector should be 4 to 6 inches long.

Tie another perfection loop in the end of your leader butt. This loop will join to the one on the connector, making leader changes quick and simple (see below).

Use blood knots to join a tippet to a knotless leader, and to join various sections of a knotted leader.

On the stream, thread the leader through the rod guides, then take a minute or two to straighten it. Pull a short section repeatedly between your fingers; the stretching and heat from the friction will remove

Tying Loops in Leader Butt and Mono Connector

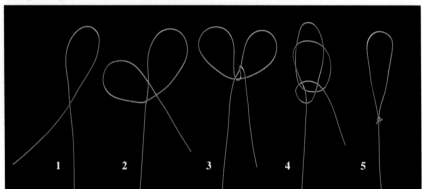

PERFECTION LOOP. (1) Make a loop by passing the free end under the standing line. (2) Wrap the free end around, to form a second loop on top of the first. (3) Wrap the free end around once more, passing it between the loops. (4) Pass the top loop through the bottom one. (5) Tighten and trim.

Loop-to-Loop Connection

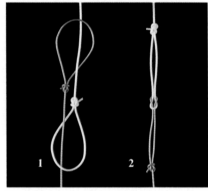

LOOP CONNECTION. (1) Pass the leader-butt loop through the loop in the fly-line connector, then run all the leader through the butt loop. (2) Snug.

Tying Tippet to Leader

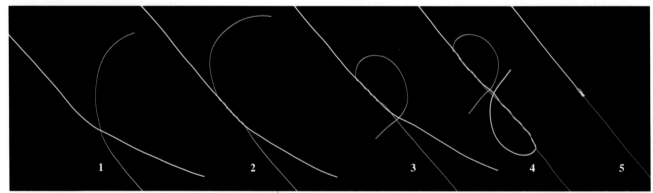

BLOOD KNOT. (1) Cross the two sections of mono. (2) With one of the ends, make four turns around the other section. (3) Bring the end back around between the two lines. (4) Repeat with the other end, inserting it in the opening so it points opposite the first end. (5) Wet the knot, then pull on the standing ends to tighten. Trim close.

the coils. Continue until the entire leader is straight. Otherwise, it won't unroll properly on the cast, and when you fish with subsurface flies the springy mono will keep you from detecting strikes.

Instead of straightening the leader with bare fingers, you can use a leader straightener (p. 58) or simply pinch it in a piece of old innertube. Then you can pull harder without cutting or burning your skin.

Always check the sharpness of your hook. Try running the point across a fingernail; it will catch in the nail if well-sharpened. Dull hooks should be touched up with a hone. Make sure the point hasn't been damaged by snagging on rocks. If it's bent slightly, you can usually straighten it with a small pair of needlenose pliers. But if any of the point is broken off, discard the fly. Many anglers flatten the barbs on their fly hooks for easier penetration, and for quicker removal with no injury to the fish.

For tying subsurface flies to your tippet, the best knot is a Duncan loop. A loop knot allows the fly to swing naturally in the current, but you can sometimes get by with a knot that draws tight on the hook eye. The Duncan loop is stronger than other loop knots, but it may tighten on the eye under the pressure of a snag or large fish. With your fingernails, you can usually slide the knot back up the line to reopen the loop.

Tie dry flies on with a double clinch knot. When tightening, make certain the knot is centered at the front of the hook eye, with the line pointing straight ahead or slightly downward. This insures the fly will float in the most natural attitude. The double clinch has two loops of line through the eye, so it won't shift during fishing, as most other knots will.

Finally, strip as much fly line off the reel as you expect to be using, then stretch it a few feet at a time, to eliminate coiling. The tendency to coil will cause snarls when you're trying to cast. Also, any waviness in the line can make it difficult to detect strikes and set the hook.

Tying Subsurface Flies to Tippet

DUNCAN LOOP KNOT. (1) Thread the tippet through the hook eye, then form a loop next to the standing line. (2) Make four to six turns around one side of the loop and the standing line. Wet the knot and (3) tighten it by pulling on the fly and the free end, then on the fly and the standing line. (4) Slide the tightened knot within ⅛ to ¼ inch of the hook eye, and pull hard on the free end with needlenose pliers to secure it there. Trim.

Tying Dry Flies to Tippet

DOUBLE CLINCH KNOT. (1) Run the tippet through the hook eye twice. (2) Make five turns around the standing line. (3) Insert the end through both loops at the eye. (4) Tighten the knot by pulling first on the standing line, then on the free end. Make sure the finished knot is centered on the hook eye. Trim.

Casting a Fly

Fly casting differs from other methods of casting in several important respects:

- Because a fly weighs so little, you cast the weight of the fly line itself, which is thicker and heavier than other kinds of line.

- Each casting stroke, forward or back, consists of two movements blended together. Using your forearm, you *load* the rod, raising the tip to start the line moving and to put a deep bend in the rod. You finish the stroke with a *wrist snap*, which forms a loop in the line and speeds it on its way.

- The keys to smooth fly casting are the proper timing and gradual acceleration of each stroke, not a sudden application of force as in spinning.

Gradual acceleration insures that the line will flow out straight on the cast. If you apply too much power

How to Make the Basic Overhead Cast

1. EXTEND about 30 feet of line. Set your feet comfortably apart, the foot on your rod side slightly back. Place your thumb on top of the grip, wrist cocked down. Point the rod low, and pull in any slack with your other hand.

2. BEGIN the backward stroke, raising your forearm smoothly but keeping your wrist cocked. The rod tip should move straight back, not swing outward in a semicircle. As the rod nears vertical, stop your arm abruptly.

3. SNAP your wrist rearward and upward (arrow), forming the loop. The unrolling line should have no waves, and the loop should be narrow. Pause until the line is nearly unrolled (dotted line), then begin the forward stroke.

too soon, the rod tip will bounce at the end of the stroke, throwing waves of slack into the line. On the following stroke, this slack will make it impossible to load the rod.

The loop formed in your line as it travels forward or rearward should be narrow, no more than 2 feet in width. A narrow loop has little air resistance, so your line travels fast without sagging to the water and with less chance of blowing off target. To form narrow loops, your wrist should break only slightly on each snap. A longer wrist movement will drop the rod tip too far, widening the loop.

Before attempting to fish, spend some time practicing on water or an open lawn. Any balanced trout outfit will do, but a 6-weight rod with a weight-forward floating line is ideal. Tie on a leader 7½ feet long and a piece of bright yarn to simulate the fly.

Start by learning the basic overhead cast. Once you have it mastered, practice false casting, shooting line and roll casting. Then you'll be ready to catch trout. The double haul is an advanced technique for distance casting, which you can learn later on. Usually, the most effective range for trout is just 25 to 40 feet.

4. PUSH your arm smoothly toward the target, accelerating gradually. Stop the arm suddenly when your rod reaches the 45-degree position. Your wrist is still bent at the same angle it took at the end of the rearward snap.

5. SNAP your wrist forward (arrow), forming a narrow loop. As before, the snap is very short but powerful. For a soft presentation, the cast should be aimed 2 or 3 feet above the spot where you want the fly to settle.

6. LOWER the rod gradually to a horizontal position as your line unrolls forward. The line will drop softly to the water. The leader should straighten completely, and the fly alight directly on the target.

71

False Casting

The false cast is a necessary supplement to the basic overhead cast. Instead of letting your line and fly settle to the water on the forward cast, you keep them in the air and make another backcast.

False casting serves several purposes:

- You can cancel an off-target cast; just pull into a backcast and correct your aim on the next cast forward.

- You can change directions from one cast to the next. It's difficult to pick your line off the water,

make a single backcast, and aim the forward cast at a target off to your side. Instead, you false-cast once in an intermediate direction and then hit the target on the next cast.

- In fishing with dry flies, a succession of false casts helps air-dry the hackle so the fly floats high and keeps its natural appearance.

- For additional distance, shoot line on a false cast. Generally, the more line you strip in on the retrieve, the more false casts it will take to cast the same distance again.

Shooting Line

Usually you will want to cast more line than you pick up from the water. If your previous cast was 40 feet long and you retrieved 15 feet while fishing the fly, you need to *shoot* line if you want to reach out more than the 25 feet you pick up. To do so,

you simply release line while the loop is in the air; the unrolling line pulls more out behind it.

Before starting a cast, make sure you have enough running line stripped off the reel. Let it lie on the water, or hold it in loose coils with your line hand. You can shoot line on a forward cast (shown below) or on a backcast.

SHOOT line by forming a large *O* with your thumb and forefinger immediately after the wrist snap on the cast. Allow loose line to flow, or shoot, through it.

BRAKE the cast as it nears the target by closing your fingers on the line. For maximum distance, you can release the line completely while shooting.

How to Roll-Cast

When obstructions prevent a normal backcast, use the roll cast. With this technique, you cannot reach

out as far as with a normal cast; the maximum distance is about 40 feet. Roll casting must be practiced on water, not land. A double-taper line works best; with a weight-forward, the running line is too light to pick up the belly.

EASE your rod tip rearward and tilt it away from you, so the line hangs outside the rod and slightly behind it. Then wait till the line stops moving.

MOVE your arm forward and downward smoothly, then make a short wrist snap. The line will roll toward the target in a wide loop and straighten.

The Double Haul

Long casts are often necessary in salmon and steelhead fishing, and occasionally in other types of trout fishing. The double haul increases line speed on the backcast and again on the forward cast, so you can make long casts and punch into the wind. This technique can increase your casting distance by 50 percent.

GRASP the line several inches ahead of the grip. Start with your rod tip low. The entire belly of the line should be extended on the water.

RAISE your line hand as you make the backcast, keeping it alongside the rod. Stop the rod suddenly as it reaches the vertical.

PULL your line hand down sharply at the instant your rod hand makes the rearward wrist snap. The pull, or haul, is only a few inches long.

BRING your line hand up near the rod as the line unrolls to the rear. If desired, you can shoot line on the backcast by forming an *O* with your fingers.

PULL down again as you make the forward stroke. This pull is longer; it begins when the rod first moves forward and ends with the wrist snap.

RELEASE the line, and hold the rod nearly level as you shoot. With a weight-forward line, it's possible to cast more than 100 feet.

Common Mistakes in Fly Casting

STARTING the backcast with the rod pointed high allows slack line to sag from the rod tip. With this slack, you cannot fully load the rod.

TURNING the arm or wrist so the reel aims outward waves the rod in a semicircle, widening line loops. The rod must go straight back and forward.

BREAKING the wrist too far rearward on the backcast widens the loop and throws the line too low behind you. Keep the wrist snap very short.

Fishing with Dry Flies

Nothing is more suspenseful than watching a big trout or salmon rise slowly to a floating fly, perhaps to reject it at the last moment or perhaps to engulf it and give you a battle demanding all your finesse.

Despite the intimidating technical discussions in books and magazines, dry-fly angling is generally the easiest way to fool a trout with a fly. It offers these advantages:

- You can read surface currents easily.

- If the trout are rising, you can see where they are and often what they're feeding on as well.

MAYFLIES

Royal Wulff Rusty Spinner March Brown

Blue Wing Olive

Hexagenia Green Drake Wulff Pale Evening Dun

STONEFLIES

Bullet Salmon Fly

Improved Sofa Pillow

CADDISFLIES

Coachman Trude

Goddard Caddis

Henryville Caddis

Elk Hair Caddis

- You know exactly where your fly is and whether it's working as it should.

- You can detect strikes by sight.

Dry flies are designed to imitate the adult stages of various aquatic insects. The classic dry, with a stiff tail and hackle and a pair of upright wings, is a good approximation of a mayfly. Stonefly imitations are similar but larger, with a single hair wing angled backward. Caddis patterns are small, like mayfly imitations, but have wings lying tentlike along the body; they are sometimes tied without hackle. Midge flies, almost microscopic, have hackle but no wings.

When selecting a dry fly on the stream, most anglers attempt to match the hatch. Recognize, however, that trout often feed selectively; and the particular insect you notice first, the biggest or most abundant species, may not be the one they want. Examine the rises and the naturals adrift on the stream to determine what the fish actually are taking. If you don't have a fly that duplicates it in size, shape, and color, settle for matching the size. An artificial slightly smaller than the real thing usually works better than one that's bigger.

Traditionally, dry-fly anglers have fished in an upstream direction. The fly drifts toward you, so you strip in line and can easily pick up the short length remaining on the water when you're ready for the next cast. Cast diagonally upstream, rather than straight up, so your leader and line won't drift over the fish and spook it. To reach difficult lies, you may want to cast across stream or downstream.

Regardless of the direction you cast, always drop your fly well upstream of the fish and let it drift into position. Remember, the rises of a fish are misleading; they do not indicate the spot where the trout actually lies (pp. 22-23).

On the drift, you must avoid drag. If the current pulls your line so the fly is dragged across the surface, the trout will refuse it and may even stop rising. Keep some slack in your leader at all times, and also in your line if needed. Use the special slack-line casts on pages 76-77. Once the line is on the water, you can mend it to maintain slack as shown on page 77. When you fish in a downstream direction, simply pay out your line as fast as the current takes it.

At times, the drag-free drift may be less productive than skating a dry fly across the surface. You do this by making a short cast downstream, then holding your rod tip high and shaking it gently from side to side while stripping in line. The fly will skip erratically on the water like a caddisfly attempting flight. The action is very different from the steady slide across the surface resulting from drag.

Dry flies often catch trout and salmon when they aren't rising, and even when no insects are hatching at all. Under these conditions you drift your fly naturally to the spots where fish are most likely to lie, or skate it over them. An effective tactic is to make several casts to a single spot, creating the illusion of a hatch.

Dry flies are used in sizes 8 to 28 for most trout, and sizes 2 to 8 for steelhead and Atlantic salmon.

Rigging Up for Dry-Fly Fishing

APPLY paste floatant to the hackle and tail of a dry fly to reduce water absorption. Rub the paste on sparingly with your fingertips.

REMOVE water or fish slime with a desiccant powder. Rub the fly gently in powder, then blow the powder away and reapply floatant.

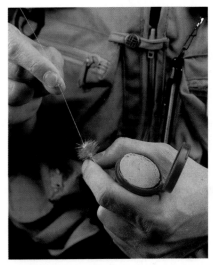

SPREAD a leader-sink compound on your tippet. A sunken tippet is less visible to trout in flat water and casts less shadow than a floating one.

How to Fish Upstream with the Pile Cast

The pile cast puts only a small amount of slack in the line, mainly near the tip, yet gives you ample slack in the leader. When you fish upstream, you need less slack in your line than in fishing across stream or downstream, because the current exerts less force on a line angled upstream.

AIM the forward cast high, parallel to the water or higher. The higher you cast, the more slack you will get on the water.

LOWER your rod tip to the water as the loop unrolls. The line and leader will straighten, then slack will develop as they fall.

DRIFT the fly over the fish. Strip in line as the fly drifts toward you. The leader and line tip should remain slack to prevent drag.

How to Fish Across Stream with the Reach Cast

This cast puts a wide upstream curve of slack in your line, doubling the length of your drift before a downstream curve, or belly, forms in the line and drag sets in. You can make a backhand reach cast (photos) or a forehand, depending on the direction of the current.

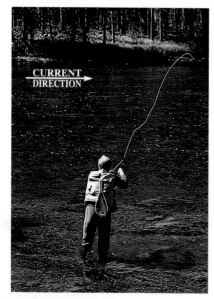

MAKE a normal forward cast, allowing some line to shoot through the guides as the loop starts to unroll toward the target.

POINT your rod tip as far as possible to the side the current is flowing from. Continue to shoot line while moving your rod to the side.

STOP the line when your fly is over the target. The line falls well upstream of the fly, so you won't have to mend so soon.

How to Fish Downstream with the S-Cast

When you fish downstream, the S-cast will put slack in your entire line, giving you a long drag-free drift. A lot of narrow S-curves work better than a few wide ones; wide curves reduce casting accuracy and are difficult to pick up from the water when you set the hook.

DIRECT the cast well above the water, shooting line. Use just enough power to reach the target, so you don't have to brake the cast.

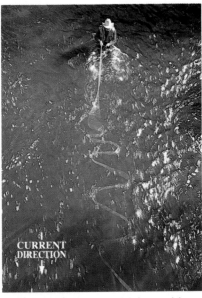

SHAKE the rod rapidly from side to side, forming curves in the line. The line must continue to shoot, or the curves will straighten.

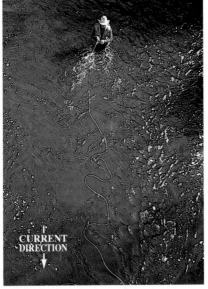

BRING the rod tip down as the line settles. The fly will drift freely until the curves wash out. You can extend the drift by paying out line.

Tips for Controlling Line

STRIP IN excess slack during a drift; press the line against the grip while pulling it in slowly with your other hand. Hold the stripped line in loose coils; if it falls on the water, the current will catch it.

MEND your line by flipping the rod tip in a semicircular motion, throwing a curve of line upstream. Make this mend before the downstream belly causes drag to set in. Repeat as often as necessary on the drift.

START each new upstream cast with a roll pickup. Make a roll cast aimed higher than usual (shown), then a normal backcast and forward cast. The fly is picked up without being pulled underwater and getting wet.

Fishing with Wet Flies

The standard wet fly has almost become a museum piece. A century ago, it was the only artificial fly in use in America; today the angler who wants a sunken fly is far more likely to tie on a streamer or nymph, which more closely resemble important trout foods such as baitfish and larval insects. Yet there are excellent reasons for using the wet fly even now, none of them sentimental.

Traditional wet-fly techniques are the simplest and most effortless in fly-fishing. There's less casting than with dry flies, so you cover the water more quickly. Also, wets are effective in fast, broken currents that would quickly drown any dry. Wet flies are generally much smaller and less air-resistant than streamers, so they're easier to cast. And your presentation and retrieve need not be as precise as in fishing with nymphs.

Wet flies have soft, absorbent hackle for quick sinking and lifelike action. The standard wet has a feather wing; dull-tinted patterns of this type are thought to represent drowned adult insects. Feather-wing wets with gaudy colors and metallic tinsels may suggest tiny baitfish, but serve mainly as attractors useful for brook trout and Atlantic salmon. Some wet patterns, called *hackle flies*, lack wings; these may resemble insect larvae or leeches.

The most popular wet flies today are specialized types. Large patterns with wings of hair or marabou, often in bright attractor colors, are commonly used for steelhead and salmon. And fat-bodied hackle flies called wooly worms, which have hackle along their entire length, are favorites for trout of all kinds on big western rivers.

Wet flies are often drifted at random, covering lots of potential holding water rather than particular lies. The wet-fly drift technique, with a floating or sink-tip line, works especially well in long runs and riffles that lack large boulders or other obvious cover. In such places, trout take shelter near small obstructions

or in depressions in the bottom that may be invisible from the surface.

You can also fish specific targets. Cast across stream and let your fly drift into the calm pockets around logs, rocks and other objects. When it reaches a pocket, feed line into the current; the fly stays where it is, but the belly expands downstream. Otherwise the fly would be swept away immediately.

An old reliable method, all but forgotten by modern anglers, is to fish with two flies at once. The second fly is tied to a dropper 3 or 4 inches long. To make the dropper, leave one of the strands untrimmed when you tie your tippet to the leader with a blood knot. Cast across stream and drift the flies to a likely spot. Then raise your rod tip and jiggle it, so the dropper fly skips on the surface while the tippet fly works underwater.

In fall and winter steelheading, it's usually necessary to fish wet flies very deep. Use the wet-fly drift with a fast-sinking shooting head or a lead-core head. Many wet flies designed for steelhead have weighted bodies or bead heads; they will bounce along bottom without snagging if the rocks are rounded.

Wet flies are used in sizes 10 to 18 for most trout, and sizes 2 to 8 for steelhead and salmon.

FEATHER WINGS — Professor, Light Cahill, Leadwing Coachman

HAIR WINGS — Green Butt Skunk, Skykomish Sunrise, Fall Favorite

HACKLE FLIES — Bread Crust, Green Soft-Hackle, Silver Soft-Hackle

PALMER HACKLE FLIES — Olive Wooly Worm, True Wooly Worm

SALMON FLIES — Silver Doctor, Jock Scott

How to Fish with the Wet-Fly Drift

CAST across stream, then let the fly swing in the current. Follow the drifting line with your rod, keeping the tip up to absorb the shock of strikes. Mend the line as it swings. Slight drag won't turn the trout off, but a wet fly dragged rapidly won't get many strikes.

RETRIEVE the fly in twitches after it swings below you. Trout usually strike at the end of the drift, as the line is straightening below you. After retrieving, take one or two steps downstream and make another cast, shooting the line you retrieved. Repeat, continuing downstream.

79

Fishing with Nymphs

Day in and day out, the odds favor the fly fisherman who uses a nymph. No matter how low or high the stream may be, no matter how cold or warm, the naturals that nymphs imitate are always present and available to the trout.

Nymphs are intended to copy the immature forms of aquatic insects, including mayflies, stoneflies, caddisflies, dragonflies, damselflies and midges. Some nymphs are close imitations of particular species, as exact as fly tiers can make them. Others are impressionistic, meant to suggest a variety of naturals in form, size and coloration. Many nymphs of both these types have bodies that are thick at the

front and thinner at the rear, simulating the wing pads and abdomen of the real thing. Usually, there's a soft, sparse hackle to serve as legs.

A nymph pattern may be tied in weighted and unweighted versions. Weighted nymphs have lead or copper wire wound onto the hook shank under the body material. They are used for fishing near bottom, especially in fast currents. Unweighted nymphs work well for fishing shallow; and because they have livelier action, many experts prefer them for fishing deep in slow water as well. To carry them deep, split-shot or lead wrap is attached to the leader. A few nymphs are designed to float, imitating the immature insect at the moment it arrives on the surface to transform into an adult.

No one becomes a complete nymph fisherman overnight. Techniques for fishing nymphs are far more numerous and varied than those for any other type of fly. Some are simple, but others are the most challenging of all ways of catching trout.

Depending on species and stage of life, the naturals may crawl across the bottom, burrow in it, swim or simply tumble along with the current. Thus the nymph fisherman can work his fly realistically by drifting

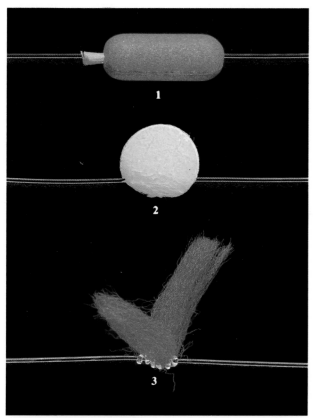

POPULAR STRIKE INDICATORS include (1) styrofoam float pegged in place with a toothpick; (2) Stay-On, which pinches onto your leader and sticks in place; and (3) colored yarn tied into a blood knot in your leader.

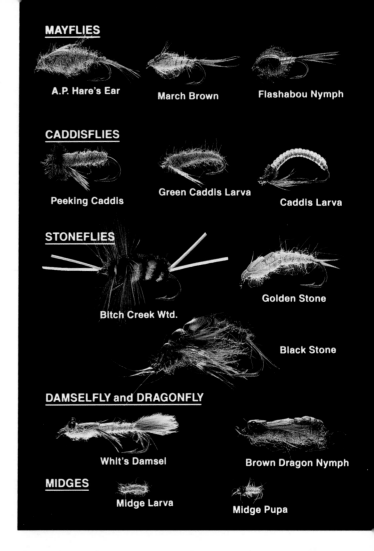

MAYFLIES

A.P. Hare's Ear — March Brown — Flashabou Nymph

CADDISFLIES

Peeking Caddis — Green Caddis Larva — Caddis Larva

STONEFLIES

Bitch Creek Wtd. — Golden Stone — Black Stone

DAMSELFLY and DRAGONFLY

Whit's Damsel — Brown Dragon Nymph

MIDGES

Midge Larva — Midge Pupa

it freely with the current, or by twitching or stripping it along at various depths.

Detecting strikes in nymph fishing can be difficult. When you use a natural drift, it's generally impossible to feel the hit. The best solution is to use a floating line with a bright-colored tip, a leader with a fluorescent butt, or some kind of strike indicator (see photo) attached to the leader. If you see any twitch or hesitation, set the hook.

For greatest sensitivity, strike indicators should be positioned as close to the fly as possible. To fish shallow, place the indicator just above the tippet knot; to fish deep, move it back toward the leader butt.

Keep your casts short so you can see the twitch more clearly. If you use a sink-tip line, keep an eye on the point where the lighter-colored floating portion disappears below the surface.

One of the easiest nymph techniques, and one of the most effective, is the wet-fly drift (p. 79). It's a good way to fish runs and riffles that lack obvious cover to cast to. By planning a drift carefully, you can also use this technique to swing your fly close to boulders or logs, or to nymphing trout you can actually see.

Sometimes these nymphing fish are visible only as flashes near the streambed as they turn and dart in the current to feed. At other times, their tails make swirls on the surface when they tip nose-down to take nymphs on the bottom, or their backs may break water when they feed on naturals that are only a few inches deep. Anglers often mistake these swirls for rises to adult insects, and make futile attempts to catch the trout with dry flies.

When drifting a nymph to a feeding fish, try to sink it exactly to the fish's eye level. To increase the depth of a drift, angle your cast farther upstream so the fly will have more time to sink before reaching the trout. Use a weighted nymph if necessary, or add a suitable amount of weight to your leader.

In the still water of pools, try making a long cast, letting the nymph sink near the bottom, then retrieving it in short twitches. In very cold water, especially in the early season, a nymph allowed to lie motionless on the bottom and twitched only occasionally may be more effective than anything else except live bait. Stay alert for strikes; a trout may pick up the loitering nymph and drop it instantly.

Nymphs used for trout range from size 1/0 to 18.

How to Fish a Nymph Upstream

MAKE a short cast upstream, so your nymph will drift to a visible fish or probable lie. If possible, cast at an angle rather than straight upstream, so your line won't drift over the fish and spook it.

STRIP line in as the current carries the nymph toward you. Let the fly drift naturally; to prevent drag, your line should have slight curves of slack. Twitch the fly when it reaches the fish or the lie.

WATCH your strike indicator closely. If it flicks or pauses at any time during the drift, set the hook instantly. Too long a delay, or too much slack in the drifting line, will cause you to miss the strike.

How to Fish a Nymph in the Surface Film

DEAD-DRIFT a nymph in smooth water. It should drift an inch or less beneath the surface, where trout feed on naturals about to emerge. To keep your fly from sinking too far, rub paste floatant on your leader, except for the last few inches of tippet. Because the leader floats, you may have to give a tug to sink the nymph. To detect strikes, watch the point where your tippet goes underwater; if more of it goes under, set the hook.

How to Fish a Current Edge with a Downstream Mend

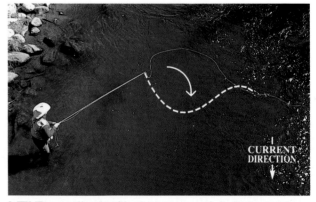

ANGLE your cast upstream into the edge of a fast current. Trout will hold in the slower water near shore, watching for nymphs to wash down in the fast current and darting out to grab them.

MEND your line by flipping a curve of slack downstream. Because the tip of the line is in the faster water, a belly forms upstream, the reverse of the usual situation. Without a mend, the fly would drift slower than the current.

MIMIC a caddis pupa rising rapidly to the surface by first (1) aiming a short cast, 25 to 30 feet, at an angle upstream; lower your rod near the water as the fly alights and the drift begins. Then (2) raise the rod tip gradually as the nymph drifts toward and alongside you. The line is lifted off the water, so no mending or retrieving is needed. As the nymph washes past you downstream, (3) lower the tip slowly. This technique gives you a drag-free drift. When the nymph is directly below you, (4) lift the tip again. The fly will dart toward the surface.

Tips for Fishing with Nymphs

APPLY floatant paste to the first 5 feet of a floating line for maximum buoyancy. To detect strikes, the line tip must stay on the surface.

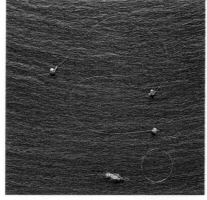

SPREAD tiny split-shot along your leader for smooth casts, rather than using one large shot. On a knotted leader, put shot just above the knots.

TIE an overhand knot around a removable split-shot before squeezing it shut. The knot keeps it from coming off during casting.

Fishing with Streamers

If you're serious about catching big trout, try fishing with streamers. The real heavyweights feed almost exclusively on baitfish; and most streamers are tied to mimic shiners, dace, sculpins, chubs, darters, and even young trout.

Not that streamers are invariably the flies to select. When the water conditions are ideal for feeding, trout show more interest in dries, nymphs and wets. Streamers produce most dependably when dries and wets don't: during periods when the water is very cold or discolored.

Pick the right times, and you may come up with a trophy. Not only do streamers attract the attention of big trout better than small flies; they also give you a better chance of hanging on once a fish is hooked. The big, stout hooks hold securely, and the heavy tippets generally used with streamers make break-offs less likely.

The traditional streamer has a wing of long hackle feathers, but other types are more popular today. Patterns with hair wings are often called *bucktails*, even if the hair is synthetic or comes from animals other than deer. Another type, the *zonker*, has a strip of soft fur tied along the top of the hook. *Muddlers* have large heads, usually of clipped deer hair, to simulate the outline of sculpins.

Some brightly colored streamers do not closely imitate any baitfish, but instead work as attractors.

How to Fish a Muddler on the Surface

TWITCH a muddler across flat water, pausing occasionally, to imitate a grasshopper or struggling baitfish. Work the fly close to grassy banks, especially near undercuts. The head and hair collar behind it should be dressed with paste floatant.

Often, these bright flies draw more strikes than realistic ones. Or trout may swirl at an attractor pattern, revealing their whereabouts, but refuse to take it. Then you can switch to a realistic streamer or some other type of fly more likely to draw a strike.

Because of their size and bulk, streamers produce more vibration than other flies when stripped through the water. This extra attraction helps fish locate them in roily water or after dark. Muddler patterns, with their oversize heads, make the most underwater disturbance.

Like nymphs, streamers are tied with or without built-in weight, and may be fished with floating or sink-tip lines, or with sinking shooting heads. Split-shot or other weight may be added to the leader as needed.

The wet-fly drift (p. 79) is a good basic technique for streamers. You can twitch the fly during the drift for a more convincing minnowlike action. Mend the line often, so the fly does not speed unnaturally through the current. Proper mending also keeps the streamer drifting broadside to the current, so it's more visible to fish lying in wait.

In slower current that does not give the fly much action, you can cast across stream, then strip the fly back toward toward you as it slowly swings downstream. No mending is needed, since the fly is retrieved before a wide belly can develop. The streamer simulates a baitfish darting across the current. Even when conditions are not ideal for streamers, this technique enables you to cover water very quickly, tempting trout to swirl at the fly as they would at an attractor pattern.

Streamers are used in sizes 1/0 to 10 for trout, sizes 1/0 to 4 for salmon.

HACKLE-WINGS

Dark Spruce

Black Ghost

Big Horn Special

BUCKTAILS

Black Nose Dace

Mickey Finn

Rainbow Trout

ZONKERS

Silver Zonker

Olive Zonker

MUDDLERS

Muddler Minnow

Spuddler

Purple Krystal Flash

How to Hang a Streamer in the Current

SWING your streamer (1) near a boulder or log. Let it hang there a minute or so, waving in the current; twitch it occasionally. 2) Shift your rod to hang the fly near another obstruction. Then, without retrieving, wade downstream; direct the streamer to other likely spots. This works well for steelhead and salmon, which often strike only if given a long look at the fly.

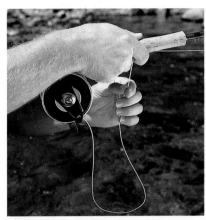

KEEP a foot of slack line between the reel and your finger when hanging a streamer in current. On a strike, you can instantly release this slack to soften the shock to the tippet.

Fishing with
Special-Purpose Flies

Historically, almost all flies were tied to imitate insects or baitfish. But anglers have come to realize the fish aren't always interested in such offerings. At times, other foods are more abundant and the trout prefer them to the everyday fare.

Certain of these morsels, such as leeches, crayfish and salmon eggs, seem to defy imitation with fur and feathers. But imaginative fly tiers have come up with realistic copies, and inventive anglers have devised techniques to bring them to life.

The most popular of these special-purpose flies are *terrestrials*. These simulate land insects such as ants, grasshoppers, crickets, beetles and inchworms, any of which may fall onto the water. Terrestrial flies are effective throughout the warm months. They're especially useful in late summer, when aquatic hatches wane. Terrestrials are fished on the surface in slow to moderate current, where the surface is relatively smooth.

Ant imitations often work better than standard dry flies on days when no trout are rising. Floating ants in sizes 18 to 22 are drifted close to the banks, where natural ants are most likely to be. These tiny flies are difficult to see, so keep your casts short and strike gently at any rise near your fly. Sinking ants are usually tied in sizes 8 to 20. Drift ant imitations with a floating line, mending often to avoid drag.

Grasshopper patterns, in sizes 4 to 14, are most productive in meadow streams, particularly on windy days when the naturals are blown onto the water. Dead-drift them along grassy banks, adding an occasional twitch. Beetles and jassids (small flat-bodied insects, also known as leafhoppers) are inconspicuous on the water, but in warm weather the trout may feed on them selectively. Beetle imitations are tied in sizes 10 to 20; jassids, sizes 16 to 22. A dead drift on the surface works best.

Leech flies are among the top lures for big trout. These are big flies, size 2 to 10. The dressings, in most cases, consist mainly of marabou or rabbit fur. These soft materials have an undulating action that matches the squirming of the naturals. Work leech flies in slow current with the wet-fly drift, twitching them from time to time. In still water, retrieve with long, slow strips; a jerky action would make the fur or marabou flare out from the hook, spoiling the illusion of a real leech.

Scud patterns imitate tiny crustaceans that are superabundant in many trout streams, especially spring creeks. Trout often gorge themselves on scuds, burrowing into weedbeds and rooting them out. It's not unusual to catch a trout that is so stuffed with scuds that it regurgitates them when you attempt to un-

hook it (photo above). When trout gorge themselves this heavily, they're tough to catch, but you may be able to draw a strike by drifting a scud pattern so it nearly hits the fish on the nose. Scud flies range from size 10 to 20.

Crayfish flies should be worked close to rocky streambeds, either drifting them with the current or

stripping them briskly through quiet water. Crayfish are most plentiful in limestone streams, and become most active in low light. A good time to fish the imitations, size 1/0 to 8, is at dusk or after dark.

In streams with runs of Pacific salmon, other salmonids like rainbows, Dolly Varden and grayling feed heavily on salmon eggs. Fly anglers take trophy fish by dead-drifting egg flies in fluorescent red, pink or orange. Use just enough weight on your leader to reach bottom; big trout may drop the fly immediately if they feel resistance. Egg patterns also are tied in white and chartreuse to imitate the spawn of suckers and other fishes.

Hair bugs, the same types used for bass, are also effective for trophy rainbows and browns, especially at night. But most bugs are too large for average-sized trout.

Effective bugs include mouse imitations (photo on opposite page), sliders and divers, in sizes 4 and 6.

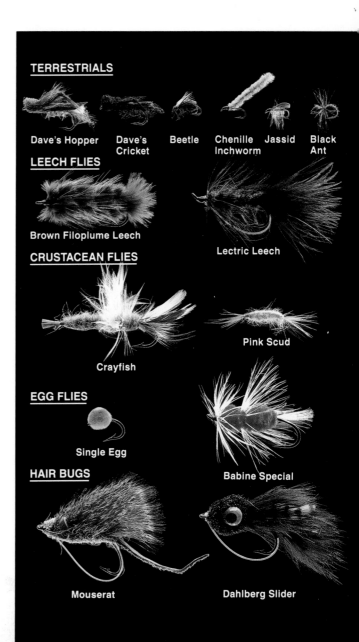

TERRESTRIALS

Dave's Hopper Dave's Cricket Beetle Chenille Inchworm Jassid Black Ant

LEECH FLIES

Brown Filoplume Leech

Lectric Leech

CRUSTACEAN FLIES

Crayfish

Pink Scud

EGG FLIES

Single Egg

Babine Special

HAIR BUGS

Mouserat

Dahlberg Slider

Spinning & Baitcasting Techniques

For the average fisherman, spinning and baitcasting are much easier than fly fishing. And in many situations, they catch more and bigger trout. Because trout eat more baitfish and fewer insects as they grow larger, good-sized baits and lures have more appeal than small flies.

The monofilament line used with spinning and baitcasting gear offers several advantages to stream fishermen. The small-diameter line cuts the current much better than fly line, so drag is not as much of a problem, and you can fish deep more easily. Mono is also less wind-resistant, which makes casting in a headwind or crosswind considerably easier. And fly line is highly visible; if you cast over a trout, or allow your line to drift ahead of the fly, the fish may spook. With mono, your presentation need not be as precise.

When heavy rains cloud a stream, fly fishing may be tough, but spinfishermen and baitcasters continue catching trout. The fish can detect the scent of natural bait or the sound and vibration of plugs and spinners.

On a narrow, brushy stream, fly casting is almost impossible because streamside obstacles foul your backcast. But with a short, ultralight spinning outfit, you can flip small lures beneath overhanging branches and fish pockets that otherwise would be difficult to reach. Spinning gear is also an advantage on wide streams because you can make long casts and cover a lot of water in a hurry.

Baitcasting gear is the best choice for exceptionally large trout and salmon. The level-wind reel eliminates the line-twist problems that plague spinfishermen when big fish strip line from their reels.

Jig Fishing

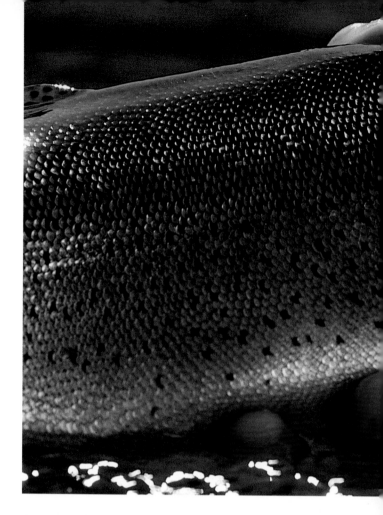

Until recently, jigs were reserved for warmwater species like bass and walleyes. Few anglers even considered using them for trout. But jigs do have a place in trout fishing, and in the hands of an expert they can be deadly.

Jigs resemble favorite trout foods such as minnows, insect larvae, crustaceans, leeches and salmon eggs. Try to match your jig color to the fish's natural food. A black or brown jig, for instance, would be a good match for most insect larvae; an orange jig, for salmon eggs.

When trout are aggressive, a jig with a tail dressing of soft plastic, marabou or hair is all you need. But when they're fussy, try tipping your jig with some type of natural bait, like a piece of worm or a small minnow.

Jigs work as well for small trout as for larger trout and salmon. They cast easily and sink rapidly in the current. A jig of the proper weight hugs bottom and is not swept by the current as much as most other lures. And jigs are versatile: you can drift them downstream, retrieve them across stream, or jig them vertically.

DOWNSTREAM DRIFTING. To catch trout feeding in riffles, cast a 1/32- to 1/80-ounce microjig upstream, then let it drift down through the riffle. Keep your rod tip high, reeling up slack as the jig drifts. Strikes may be hard to detect, but you can attach a strike indicator (inset photo below), just as you would in nymph fishing.

For casting these tiny jigs, use a 4½- to 5½-foot ultralight spinning rod with a slow to medium action. Spool your reel with limp, 2- to 4-pound mono.

CROSS-STREAM RETRIEVE. In deeper water, use a heavier jig, 1/16 to 1/4 ounce. Quarter your cast upstream, aiming for targets like boulders and logs. Let the jig sink to bottom, then retrieve in a series of short twitches, lowering the jig back to bottom with a taut line after each twitch. If the bottom-bouncing technique doesn't pay off, try a twitching retrieve in the mid-depths and just beneath the surface. Sometimes a faster retrieve will trigger a strike.

With these heavier jigs, use a medium-power, fast-action spinning rod, from 5¼ to 6 feet in length, with limp 4- to 8-pound mono.

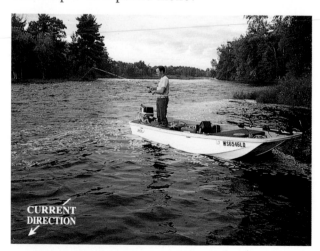

90

VERTICAL JIGGING. This technique works well for salmon and large trout in deep pools and runs of good-sized rivers. Simply lower a jig or jigging spoon to bottom, then jig vertically as the boat drifts downstream. Keep your line taut as the lure sinks; set the hook at the slightest tug. Use a lure weighing from ⅜ ounce to 2 ounces, depending on current speed and water depth.

A heavy baitcasting outfit works best for vertical jigging. Use a 5½- to 6-foot, fast-action rod with 12- to 20-pound mono. For salmon, you may need mono up to 30-pound test.

CURRENT DIRECTION

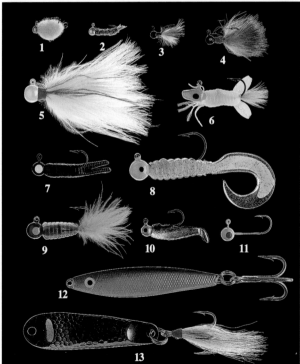

POPULAR JIGS and jigging lures include (1) Glo-Ball, (2) Chenille Grub, (3) Mini Marabou, (4) Rabbit Hair, (5) marabou jig, (6) Foxee Jig™, (7) Beetle™, (8) Teeny™, (9) Fuzz-E-Grub, (10) Sassy Shad™, (11) plain jig head, (12) Nördic™, (13) Hopkins® Spoon.

Casting with Hardware

The term "hardware" means all hard-bodied lures like spoons, spinners and plugs. Hardware attracts trout by flash and vibration. By casting with hardware, you can cover a lot of water in a hurry. The technique works best from late spring through early fall, when higher water temperatures make trout more aggressive.

Compared to most other trout-fishing techniques, hardware fishing is easy. Simply cast across stream, then regulate the speed of your retrieve so the lure ticks bottom. When trout are actively feeding, ticking bottom may not be necessary; the fish will swim upward to grab the lure.

Exactly how you angle your cast depends on the lure, the water depth and the current speed. The more you angle it upstream, the deeper the lure will run. If the lure is bouncing bottom too much, angle the cast farther downstream. This way, water resistance from the current will keep the lure off bottom.

Standard spinners and thin spoons are popular in small streams, where distance casting is not important. Sonic spinners, which have a shaft that passes through the blade, are extremely popular in the West. The blade starts turning at a very low retrieve speed.

Weight-forward spinners and medium to thick spoons are a better choice in bigger rivers or in those with deep water or fast current. These heavier lures can be cast much farther, and they run deeper.

Floating minnow plugs work well in small streams, but sinking minnow plugs and diving crankbaits are more effective in deeper current.

With spinners, spoons and sinking minnow plugs, the slower you retrieve, the deeper the lures will run. Floating minnow plugs and crankbaits run deepest with a medium to medium-fast retrieve.

For casting spinners, small spoons and minnow plugs, use a 5- to 6-foot light spinning outfit with 2- to 6-pound mono; for larger spoons and diving plugs, a 5½- to 7-foot, medium-power spinning outfit with 6- to 8-pound mono. Steelhead and salmon fishermen often use 8- to 9-foot, medium- to heavy-power spinning rods with 8- to 17-pound mono.

To avoid line twist, attach spinners and spoons with a small ball-bearing snap-swivel. Or, splice in a swivel about 6 inches ahead of the lure. Attach minnow plugs with a small snap or a Duncan loop knot; crankbaits, with a snap or a double clinch knot (p. 69).

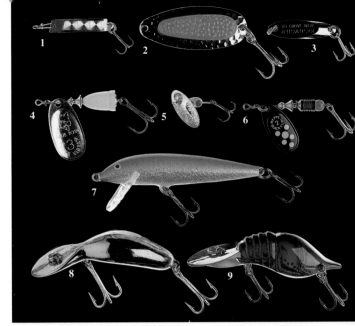

HARDWARE includes spoons like (1) Super Duper®, (2) Pixee™, (3) Kastmaster®; spinners like (4) Super Vibrax®, (5) Panther Martin®, (6) Black Fury®; plugs like (7) Countdown Rapala®, (8) Tadpolly®, (9) Crawdad®.

Tips for Casting Hardware

HANG your lure in the current to fish hard-to-reach pockets such as holes beneath log jams, brush piles, overhanging limbs or undercut banks. From an upstream position, cast just short of the pocket, let out a little line, then allow the current to work your lure.

CRANK a floating minnow plug through a riffle in early morning or late evening to catch feeding trout. From a downstream position, cast to the head of the riffle, then reel rapidly through the riffle and downstream run. After a few casts, move to the next riffle.

WORK the cover farthest downstream and closest to you first. Then, a hooked fish will not spook others in unfished water when the current sweeps it downstream, or in unfished water close to you when you reel it in. Make your casts in the order shown in the photo.

93

Trolling

When you troll, your lure is in the water all the time, maximizing your chances of catching fish. Trolling offers several other advantages over casting: it's an easier technique for the novice; it enables you to cover more water; and where multiple lines are legal, you can troll with several lures at once.

Trolling works best in big rivers that have long stretches of deep water with slow to moderate current. It's not well-suited to river stretches with lots of riffles or rapids, and not recommended for shallow or very clear water. Because the boat passes over the fish before the lure arrives, spooking may be a big problem. You can reduce spooking by trolling in S-curves. This way the lure does not track continuously in the boat's wake.

Another way to avoid spooking fish is to troll with side planers (photo above). These devices attach to your line, pulling it well to the side of the boat's wake. They also let you cover a wider swath of water. Another way to fish side planers is to walk along shore, using the planer to carry your line to midstream waters you couldn't reach by casting.

Equipment for Trolling

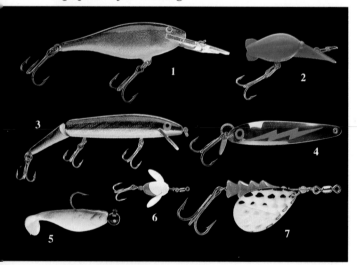

POPULAR LURES for trolling include (1) Shad Rap™, (2) Hot Shot®, (3) Jointed Minnow/Floater®, (4) Flutter Laker Taker®, (5) Sassy Shad™, (6) Spin-N-Glo®, (7) Skagit Special®.

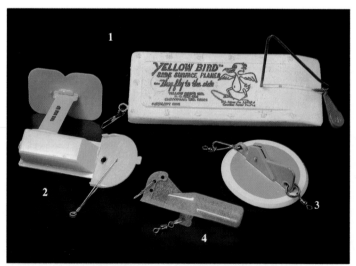

SIDE PLANERS include (1) Yellow Bird; (2) Hot Shot® Side Planer; (3) Dipsey Diver®, a weighted diving plane that also pulls to the side; and (4) Jet Diver, an unweighted diving plane.

Diving planes also attach to your line, taking the lure deep. The unweighted type is all you need in most streams; weighted ones generally run too deep.

You can troll for practically any salmonid, but the technique is used most often for anadromous fishes like steelhead and Pacific salmon.

Baitcasting gear works best for trolling. A good trolling rod is 7 to 9 feet long, stiff enough to handle the water resistance against the lure, but light enough at the tip to telegraph the lure's action. Use abrasion-resistant mono, from 6- to 20-pound test depending on the size of the fish. A depth finder helps you follow breaks in the bottom contour.

Most anglers troll with deep-diving crankbaits. You can also use minnow plugs, spoons, jigs, and spinner-and-bait combinations. It's a good idea to keep your lures near bottom, except when trout are feeding on insects or salmon smolts and will come up for a lure. Pacific salmon and steelhead feed very little in streams, but may strike a deep-running crankbait out of irritation or in defense of their territory. Normally, no extra weight is needed to get a crankbait to bottom, but you may have to add weight to other lures.

Trolling styles used in stream fishing for trout and salmon include: slipping, upstream trolling and downstream trolling.

SLIPPING. The term "slipping" means letting the boat drift slowly downstream, reducing its speed with a motor or oars while allowing the lures to trail in the current. As long as the boat drifts more slowly than the current, the force of the water will give the lures action. Some trout fishermen refer to this technique as "backtrolling."

To cover wide channels, zigzag your boat while slipping. This allows you to cover more water on the drift, a big advantage if you don't have a motor. It also gives your lures more action, causing them to speed up and slow down, rise and fall.

Slipping is effective year around, but works especially well in cold water; the slow-moving lure appeals to lethargic fish. The technique has one major advantage over other trolling methods: the lure passes over the fish before the boat does, so they're less likely to spook.

UPSTREAM TROLLING. You can troll upstream only in slow current. Otherwise, water resistance is so great that the lure is forced to the surface. Where the current is slow enough, you can troll upstream, then turn around and troll back down, keeping your lures in the water.

DOWNSTREAM TROLLING. This technique is often used to present spinners or other lures that do not require much current for good action. Trolling downstream slightly faster than the current gives these lures enough action, yet they look like drifting food. To troll slowly enough, you may have to shift your motor between forward and neutral every few seconds. When using lures like spoons and crankbaits, you will have to troll somewhat faster.

By trolling downstream, you are in a better position to fight the fish. The current pushes a hooked fish in the direction the boat moves, reducing the possibility of breaking the line or tearing out the hooks.

How to Use a Side Planer

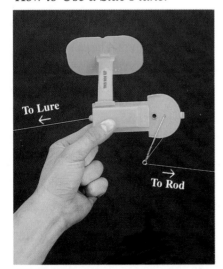

ATTACH the planer to your line after letting out about 50 to 75 feet. Different planers attach differently; refer to the directions.

LET OUT more line; the planer will start to move laterally from the boat. Continue feeding line until the planer is 50 to 75 feet to the side.

LOCK your reel, check the drag, and place your rod in a holder. If desired, let out another planer on the opposite side of the boat.

95

STANDARD BUBBLE RIGS work best for casting across stream or downstream; if fished upstream, the bubble would drift ahead of the fly. Tie the rig by threading a plastic bubble on your line, then attaching a dry fly, wet fly, streamer or nymph. Twist the ends of the bubble so it locks in place a foot up the line. With a dry fly, you can put a little water in the bubble for casting weight; use a drag-free drift. With a sinking fly, you can fill the bubble with water or add split-shot for more depth; dead-drift the fly or twitch it for extra action.

Spinfishing with Flies

Even if you don't own a fly rod, you can fly-fish with spinning gear. In fact, spinning with flies works better in some situations. In deep water, for instance, you can attach split-shot to mono line and reach bottom more easily than with fly line. And in high winds, mono is easier to control.

In streams with flies-only regulations, spinning gear is usually legal, as long as the lure is a fly. But to cast a fly, you must attach some extra weight.

With a sinking fly, simply add a split-shot or two about a foot up the line. Leader wrap, lead sleeves or a good-sized strike indicator will also add weight. Strike indicators help detect light pickups as well.

Dry flies and sinking flies can be rigged with a weighted float or a plastic bubble, which can be partially filled with water for extra casting weight. If you use a clear float or bubble, trout will pay little attention to it. But a float or bubble splashing down close to a fish, or drifting over it ahead of the fly, may cause it to spook.

A long, soft rod is best for casting flies and manipulating them in the water. A stiff rod doesn't flex enough to cast a light weight, and could snap a light leader when you set the hook. A 6½- to 7½-foot, slow-action spinning rod or an 8½- to 9½-foot, 4- to 6-weight fly rod with a spinning reel is a good choice. Spool your reel with 2- to 8-pound, limp mono.

Many spinfishermen use line that is too heavy, and add too much weight, inhibiting the movement of the fly. Always use the lightest line practical for the conditions, and the lightest weight that will allow you to cast and reach the desired depth. Too much weight causes snagging problems; and even with minimal weight, strikes are more difficult to detect than with fly-fishing gear.

Other Rigs for Spinfishing with Flies

MAKE a (1) dropper rig by tying a blood knot 2 feet up your line, leaving a 1-foot tag end. Tie a float or bubble to the line, a dry fly or terrestrial to the dropper. This rig works best for casting upstream. Make a (2) split-shot rig by pinching shot 6 to 12 inches above the fly.

How to Fish a Dropper Rig

QUARTER your cast upstream above a rise, then raise your rod so the fly just reaches the water. Drift the fly over the rise, making sure you keep the float out of the fish's window. Occasionally lift the rod to dabble the fly on the surface.

Tips for Spinfishing with Flies

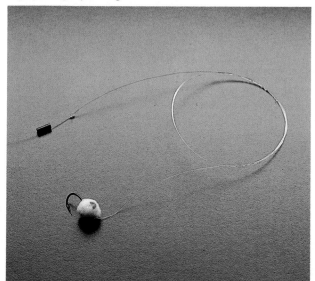

USE a leader sleeve instead of split-shot when fishing on a snaggy bottom. The cylindrical sleeve slips along bottom better than a round split-shot. Slide the sleeve onto your line, then tie on a leader; the knot acts as a stop.

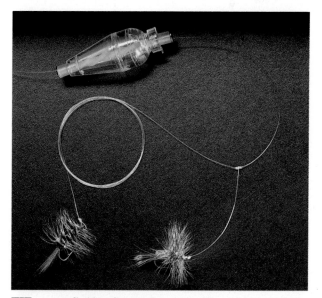

TIE a wet-fly/dry-fly rig for use with a plastic bubble. Make a dropper by tying a blood knot, leaving a 3-inch tag end. Tie a dry fly to the dropper; it doubles as a strike indicator. Tie a wet fly to the end of the line.

Natural Bait

Fly-fishing purists frown on the idea of using spoons, spinners and other hardware to catch trout, and the idea of using natural bait is even farther down their list of tolerable tactics. But there's no denying that natural bait catches lots of trout; in fact, there are times when it badly outfishes flies and hardware.

Trout and salmon rely on their sense of smell to a greater extent than most other gamefish. They can detect dissolved substances in minute concentrations, as evidenced by the ability of sea-run salmon and steelhead to return to their home stream on the basis of its unique odor. So it's not surprising that they use their remarkable sense of smell to help them find food.

Natural bait appeals to this highly developed sense. Smell is especially important during periods of high, muddy water. Under these conditions, trout cannot see flies or hardware, but they can easily detect the odor of natural bait.

In early spring, when the water is still cold and few insects are hatching, natural bait usually outproduces flies by a wide margin. Natural bait is also a good choice in streams that do not have many insects. And big trout or those in heavily fished streams can be super-wary, closely inspecting any potential food item. They're likely to recognize any imitation as a fake.

Bait fishermen often make the mistake of using heavy line and a big hook, then adding a heavy sinker and a golfball-sized bobber. This type of rig is fine for northern pike, but will seldom catch a trout. For most stream trout, bait-fishing specialists use light spinning tackle with 2- to 4-pound mono, size 6 to 12 hooks, and a split-shot for weight. Of course large trout and salmon require heavier tackle, but seldom will you need line heavier than 8-pound test or a hook larger than size 2.

The major drawback of natural bait is the problem of deep hooking. Even a small trout often takes the bait so deeply it's impossible to remove the hook without causing serious injury. If you plan on releasing your trout, don't use live bait. If you must release a deeply hooked trout, cut the line rather than trying to remove the hook.

Another disadvantage of many natural baits is the difficulty of keeping them alive and carrying them, especially if you're wading. And in some states, certain natural baits, like minnows, are illegal for trout.

The variety of trout and salmon baits is nearly endless. Garden worms, nightcrawlers and salmon eggs are the most common baits, along with minnows and cut fish. Leeches, adult and larval insects, and crayfish are not as popular, but are no less effective. Fishermen have also discovered that certain "grocery baits," like marshmallows and corn, work extremely well, especially for stocked trout.

Although most trout will take any of these baits, some have a distinct preference. Also, a given bait may be more productive at certain times of year or under certain water conditions. Following are details on the most common live baits used for trout:

GARDEN WORMS. Any trout will take a worm. The bait is effective anytime, but works best in early spring when streams are high and discolored. For convenience, carry your worms in a box that attaches to your belt (p. 103).

Push a size 6 to 10 hook through the middle of the worm, letting the ends dangle; or hook the worm two or three times, letting the tail dangle (photo, opposite page).

NIGHTCRAWLERS. You can use nightcrawlers and garden worms interchangeably; for small trout, half a crawler is better than a whole one. Crawlers must be kept cooler than garden worms.

Push a size 6 or 8 hook through the broken end of a half crawler (top), or through the middle of a whole crawler (bottom). Or, hook the crawler two or three times, like a garden worm.

MINNOWS. Trout fishermen commonly use fathead minnows and shiners because of their availability, but almost any kind of minnow in the 1½- to 3-inch range will work. Minnows catch trout year around, but are most effective in spring and early summer, when young baitfish are most numerous. Live minnows are best in slow-moving water; in current, dead ones work nearly as well.

Trout, particularly browns, eat more fish as they grow older, so minnows are a good choice for the big ones.

Sculpins, often called bullheads by mistake, are the prime bait for trophy browns in numerous western streams. But other baitfish are illegal in most western states, and many other states ban any type of baitfish. These regulations are intended to prevent introduction of non-native fish species, and to reduce the trout harvest. Always check your local fishing regulations before using any kind of baitfish.

To carry minnows when you're wading, put them in a small bucket with a perforated lid, then tie the bucket to your waders. Fatheads are the easiest to keep alive.

Most minnows are hooked through the lips with a size 4 or 6 short-shank hook. You can also hook a sculpin by pushing a size 4 or 6 double-needle hook through the vent and out the mouth (photo above), then attaching a special clip to the front of the hook.

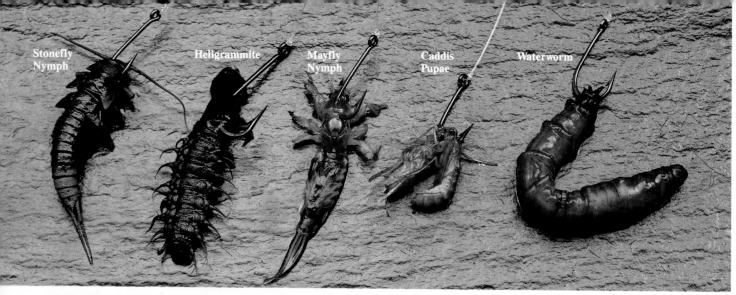

Stonefly Nymph   Hellgrammite   Mayfly Nymph   Caddis Pupae   Waterworm

AQUATIC INSECTS. Immature aquatic insects work better than adults, mainly because they're easier to keep on the hook. Stonefly nymphs and hellgrammites (dobsonfly larvae) top the list, but mayfly nymphs, caddis larvae, waterworms (cranefly larvae) and other immature forms also catch trout.

Any of these baits will take trout year around, but stonefly nymphs are best in midsummer; hellgrammites, in spring and early summer. You can find stonefly nymphs clinging to the undersides of rocks and logs in cold streams; hellgrammites are found in warmer water, and can be caught by turning over rocks in a riffle while someone holds a small-mesh seine just downstream. Mayfly nymphs can be found by sifting through mud on the stream bottom; waterworms, by digging through sticks and debris on the bottom or in a beaver dam; caddisworms, by checking the undersides of rocks.

Adult aquatic insects are not as common in a trout's diet as larval forms. But some adults, such as stoneflies, make good trout bait. Watch for them as you walk along the stream, and don't hesitate to give them a try.

Stonefly nymphs should be hooked through the collar with a size 8 or 10 light-wire hook; hellgrammites, under the collar with a size 4 to 8 hook; mayfly nymphs, through the hard plate just behind the head with a size 10 or 12 light-wire hook; caddis pupae (shown in photo) or larvae, by pushing a size 12 to 16 light-wire hook through the head or threading it through the body (use several larvae or pupae, or a larva inside its case); waterworms, through the tough skin just ahead of the tail lobes using a size 8 or 10 light-wire hook. Adult mayflies and stoneflies (not shown) stay on best when hooked through the head with a size 10 or 12 light-wire hook.

Grasshopper

Cricket

Waxworms

TERRESTRIAL INSECTS. In late summer, trout often lie near the bank, waiting for grasshoppers to get blown into the water. Where hoppers are plentiful, you can easily catch them by hand or with a small insect net. They can be fished alive or dead, floating or submerged. Crickets are not used as widely, but are equally effective.

Fishermen have discovered that waxworms (bee moth larvae), maggots (fly larvae) and other larval baits used for ice fishing are excellent for trout. They work particularly well in winter, when most other baits are hard to find. Their small size is an advantage when the water is cold and trout feeding slows.

Hoppers and crickets are hooked with a size 6 to 10 light-wire hook, either under the collar (left photo, top), or through the body so the point protrudes from the underside of the abdomen (left photo, middle). Waxworms and maggots are hooked through the head with a size 10 or 12 light-wire hook (left photo, bottom); some anglers hook on two or three.

Crayfish Taii

Scuds

Crayfish

Mud Shrimp

CRUSTACEANS. Crayfish from 1½ to 3 inches long make good summertime bait for big trout, especially browns. For smaller trout, use only the tail. Crayfish work best in streams with high crayfish populations.

You can catch crayfish by quickly grabbing them after turning over rocks in the streambed. Or, use the seining technique on page 103. Try to select crayfish in the softshell stage. Live crayfish can be hooked through the tail, from the bottom up, with a size 2 to 4 hook. Crayfish tails are hooked the same way.

Mud shrimp and ghost shrimp are actually soft-bodied crabs. They are popular for steelhead and salmon in Pacific coastal streams, particularly in spring and summer. They average about 5 inches in length, so they are not likely to catch small trout.

Rig the shrimp on a 1/0 plastic-worm hook with an egg loop (p. 107). Push the hook through the top of the tail and out the bottom, bring the point through the body from the bottom up, then cinch the egg loop over the tail. Tie a small piece of yarn to the egg loop for attraction and to open the loop when rebaiting.

You can buy mud shrimp at bait shops or catch them on tidal flats with a clam tube, a device used to suck them out of their burrows. Keep them alive in a container with an inch of water or a layer of moist weeds, sawdust or paper towels.

Scuds, small crustaceans found among submerged weeds, are commonly eaten by trout but seldom used for bait, because they are difficult to keep on the hook. The best way is to thread them on a size 12 or 14 light-wire hook, two or three at a time.

EGGS. All species of trout and salmon feed on each other's eggs. Salmon eggs are most popular for bait because of their large size and commercial availability, but trout eggs also work well.

A single egg will catch anything from an 8-inch brook trout to a 50-pound chinook. But for salmon and large trout, most anglers prefer egg clusters, either plain or tied in a mesh spawn bag. Eggs are effective year around, but they work best during and after a spawning run, when the fish are eating eggs.

Fresh salmon eggs deteriorate quickly, but you can preserve them by rolling them in powdered borax or soaking them in a boric-acid solution.

To hook a single egg (1) pierce one edge with a size 10 to 14 salmon-egg hook, (2) slide the egg up the shank, (3) turn it 180 degrees, then (4) push it down so the point is buried.

Attach a spawn chunk by tying an egg loop (p. 107) on a size 4 to 8 hook with a turned-up eye, putting a chunk of spawn into the loop, then tightening.

SPAWN BAG. (1) Wrap eggs in a 2- to 3-inch square of nylon mesh or a piece of nylon stocking. Gather the corners of the mesh; the bag should be ⅜ to ⅝ inch in diameter. (2) Wrap five loops of thread around the mesh, and secure the bag with a series of half-hitches. Put the finished bags in a jar of borax, then shake the jar. Refrigerate for up to two weeks, or freeze. (3) To hook a spawn bag, push a size 4 to 8 short-shank hook through the bag so only the eye and point are exposed (inset).

YARN FLY. Salmon and steelhead anglers often drift-fish with a spawn bag and yarn fly. To make a yarn fly, (1) pass the line through a turned-up-eye hook, then tie a *snell*. (2) Make a loop in the line you passed through, and hold it against the hook shank. (3) Wrap the free end through the loop about five times, and (4) snug up by pulling on the free end and standing line. (5) Place a short piece of yarn under the line between the snell and the eye, then (6) pull the line to secure the yarn. Hook the spawn bag.

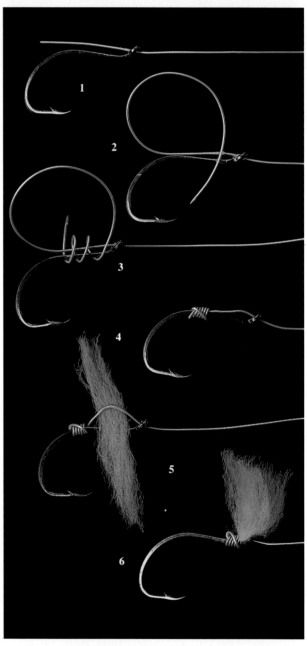

GROCERY BAITS. Though unappealing to many fishermen, grocery baits such as whole-kernel corn, small marshmallows, and soft cheese like Velveeta® catch lots of trout. Single corn kernels and small marshmallows are simply pushed onto a size 8 or 10 hook. Soft cheese can be molded around the hook. Grocery baits may suggest the pellets that stocked trout have been fed in hatcheries. They work best for trout that have been recently stocked; they are not as effective on wild trout.

CONTAINERS for live bait include (1) small minnow bucket, which straps to your waders or vest and has a perforated lid that allows easy exchange of water; (2) plastic box that dispenses one small bait at a time, ideal for hoppers; (3) metal worm box that attaches bottom-up to your belt, and flips over to open so the worms will be on top; and (4) egg dispenser, which attaches to your belt and has a flip-top lid so you can quickly grab an egg.

Tips for Catching and Keeping Natural Baits

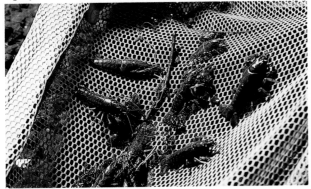

CATCH crayfish by holding a small-mesh seine on bottom just downstream of a rocky riffle. When another person turns over rocks, crayfish wash into the net. Keep them in a minnow bucket filled with cool water.

DIG through silt, leaves and sticks on a muddy bottom or in a beaver dam to find burrowing larvae such as waterworms and mayfly nymphs. Keep them cool in a container filled with damp leaves or moss.

How to Preserve Salmon Eggs

CUT an egg skein into ½- to ¾-inch squares, leaving the membrane attached. Drop the squares into powdered, non-detergent borax.

ROLL the squares in borax until thoroughly coated. Borax preserves the eggs, but washes off in water so the eggs retain their natural scent.

PLACE the squares in a small jar with a layer of borax on the bottom. Cover and shake to coat the squares again. Refrigerate or freeze.

Drift Fishing

Drift fishing accounts for more trout and salmon than any other bait-fishing technique. The idea is to present your bait so it drifts naturally with the current, just like real food.

You can drift-fish for everything from small brookies to trophy steelhead and salmon. The basic technique is the same; only the gear is different.

Position yourself to the side and just downstream of a riffle or run likely to hold trout. Most pools do not have enough current to keep your bait drifting. Before casting, look for boulders, logs or other likely cover, then quarter your cast upstream so the bait will skirt the object as it drifts.

Light spinning gear works best for average-sized trout. A 6- to 7-foot, medium-action rod is long enough for good line control, yet flexible enough for lobbing delicate baits. The lighter the line you use, the easier it is to achieve a drag-free drift. Heavy line has more water resistance, so the current creates a larger belly and the bait begins to drift too fast. Limp, clear, 4-pound mono is a good all-around choice, but you may need heavier line if the bottom is snaggy.

Some drift fishermen use a fly rod with a spinning reel. The longer rod gives them even better line control and makes it easier to dunk the bait into hard-to-reach spots.

Steelhead and salmon anglers commonly use 8- to 10-weight fly rods, and fly reels loaded with 8- to 17-pound abrasion-resistant mono. With a rod this long, you can drift your bait, usually a spawn bag or some type of spawn imitation, through narrow runs with perfect control. Simply swing the bait upstream, walk it through the run, then swing it upstream again. This repetitious presentation is the best way to entice a strike from fish that aren't really feeding.

In drift fishing, it's important to select a sinker of the proper weight. Too heavy, and it will hang on bottom so the bait cannot drift as fast as the current. Too light, and the current will lift the bait off bottom. You must choose a sinker heavy enough that it just ticks bottom as the bait drifts. Carry a selection of sinkers and split-shot in various sizes, and use different ones to suit the conditions.

Almost any natural bait tough enough to stay on the hook will work for drift fishing. A delicate bait like an adult mayfly would probably tear off. You can add visual appeal by snelling a small piece of fluorescent yarn on your hook just ahead of the bait (p. 102). In fact, many steelhead and salmon anglers use only the yarn.

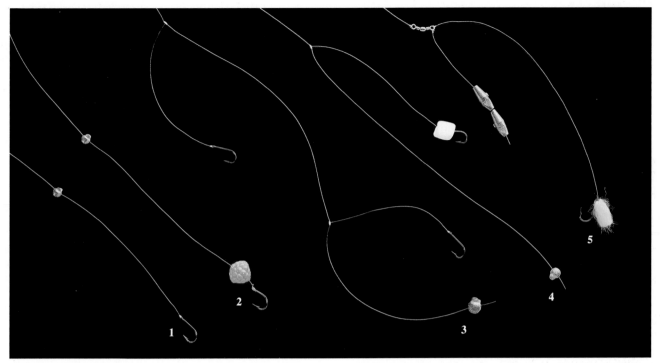

DRIFT-FISHING RIGS include: (1) basic split-shot rig; (2) split-shot rig with drift bobber for extra attraction and for keeping bait off bottom; (3) double-dropper rig for fishing with two baits. The split-shot pulls off when snagged; (4) marshmallow rig for floating bait off bottom; and (5) drift-sinker rig with yarn fly.

Basic Drift-Fishing Technique

STRIP off enough line to reach your casting target, hold the slack in your free hand, then bring the rod back over your shoulder.

QUARTER your cast upstream into a run or deep riffle. Use a gentle lobbing motion. Do not snap the rod or you will tear the bait off the hook.

KEEP your rod tip high and follow the bait as it drifts downstream. Take up slack with your free hand as the angle of your line changes.

SET the hook whenever the bait stops moving. When you reach the end of your drift and current begins to lift the bait, strip in line and cast again.

Float Fishing

Floating is an easy way to fish a river too deep for wading. It also allows you to fish remote stretches of rivers, or reaches where access is denied because of private lands. Floating is especially popular for steelhead and salmon in big rivers, but you can float-fish for any kind of trout.

Drag causes the same problems in drift-fishing with natural bait (p. 104) as it does in fly fishing. After you cast, the current puts a belly in your line and soon increases the speed of your bait so it appears unnatural to the fish. The belly also makes it harder to detect strikes.

But with the boat floating at the same speed as the current, drag is virtually eliminated. One common method of float fishing is simply to lower some type of natural bait to bottom and let the boat do the rest. Floating also gives you a longer drag-free drift when fly casting.

You do not have to cast when floating with bait, so you can use fairly heavy tackle if necessary. Steelhead and salmon fishermen commonly use medium to heavy baitcasting gear with 8- to 17-pound mono. With no casting, there is less wear and tear on the bait, and it stays in the water more of the time.

Should you hook a big trout or salmon while float fishing, you can follow it with the boat, guiding it away from obstacles and greatly increasing your chances of landing it.

Most float fishing is done from a shallow-draft boat, but even then you must pay close attention to stream conditions. If the water is low, the boat will scrape rocks and get hung up in shallow riffles. In high water, you must watch for dangerous rapids and stay away from flooded trees along the bank.

FLOATING keeps the line drifting at the same speed as the boat, so the line stays straight and the bait drifts natur-ally. When drift-fishing (inset), the current forms a belly in your line, speeding up the drift.

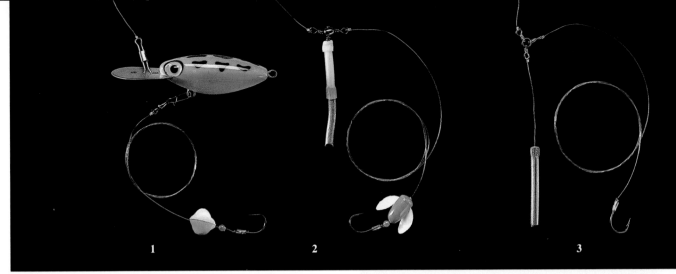

RIGS for float fishing include (1) diver rig, which pulls your bait deep and gives it an erratic action. Remove the hooks from a diving plug, then add a 3-foot trailer with a drift bobber and egg cluster (not shown) at the rear.

(2) Surgical-tubing rig, which allows pencil lead to pull out when snagged. Spin-N-Glo® adds color and flotation. (3) Three-way swivel rig with the pencil lead pinched on. Lead will pull off on snag if not pinched too tight.

How to Tie an Egg Loop

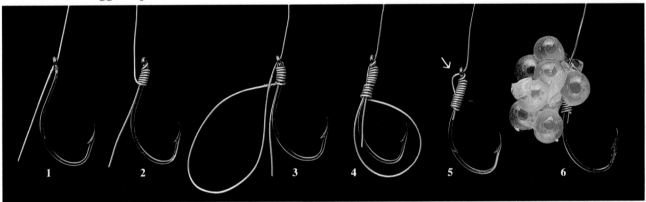

THREAD (1) the end of a 24-inch piece of mono through a hook with a turned-up eye. (2) Wrap the long end around the shank and tag end six to eight times. (3) Make a loop, then push the long end back through the eye. (4) Hold the wrapped portion while making six to eight more

wraps over the tag end and the other line. (5) Pull on the long end to snug up the knot; trim the tag end. Push the line back through the eye to open a loop, then (6) insert the eggs and pull on the line to secure them. Tie the line to a pencil-lead rig.

Tips for Float Fishing

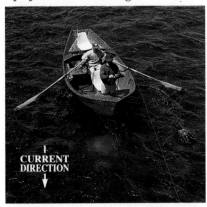

SLOW the drift of your boat to work the water thoroughly. Point the stern upstream and row while another angler works his bait off the bow. This technique is called *back bouncing*.

PULL your boat up on shore, then get out and wade for better coverage of a specific spot. Many anglers float-fish the area between riffles, but wade to fish the riffles themselves.

AVOID *sweepers*, trees and branches projecting horizontally from shore. During high water, fast current could wash you under a sweeper and overturn your boat instantly.

Freelining

If you stand along a grassy bank on a hot summer's day, you may see trout rising to take grasshoppers and other insects that fall into the stream.

When trout are feeding this way, you can catch them by freelining with the insects they are eating. Most fishermen freeline with light spinning gear, but you can also use a fly rod, with either a floating fly line or monofilament. The long rod helps to position the nearly weightless bait over the lie. The technique is simple: attach the bait to a light-wire hook, stand upstream of the lie, then pay out line. With fly-casting gear or light spinning gear, you can also flip the bait upstream and let it float down. Because there is no sinker, the bait will float on the surface or just beneath it.

Freelining works best in late summer, when adult insects are numerous and stream levels low. Any insect-eating trout are susceptible to the technique. The best area for freelining is along a grassy bank or other spot where insects cling to streamside vegetation and commonly fall into the water.

On a small, overgrown stream where casting is impossible, you can use a leaf to freeline a split-shot rig into a deep hole. Without the leaf, the rig would hang up in the shallower water above.

How to Float Bait on a Leaf

BALANCE a split-shot rig and bait on a leaf large enough to support their weight. The split-shot should be attached no more than a few inches from the bait.

OPEN your bail and feed line so the leaf and rig float downstream toward a deep hole. Twitch the line when the leaf reaches the hole; the rig will fall off and sink.

Plunking

Practically every experienced trout fisherman has been badly outfished at some time or other by a kid plunking worms into a pool. While the technique is not glamorous, it accounts for plenty of trout.

The term plunking simply means still-fishing. The usual technique is to attach a sinker to the line, bait up, lob-cast into a pool, then sit back and wait.

Plunking works especially well for big trout. If you sit quietly, they eventually detect the scent and swim over to investigate. If you continually cast and retrieve, you are likely to spook them.

Almost any live bait will work, but nightcrawlers and minnows are most popular. In stocked streams, anglers often plunk with Velveeta® cheese and other junk food. Browns, rainbows and cutthroat seem most susceptible to plunking.

Use only enough weight to keep your bait from drifting. If you attach a heavy sinker, the fish will feel resistance and spit the bait. In small streams, a split shot is normally adequate, but in bigger streams, you may need a small slip sinker. Most anglers plunk with light spinning gear and 4- to 8- pound mono, depending on the size of the trout and the snaginess of the bottom.

Plunking Tips

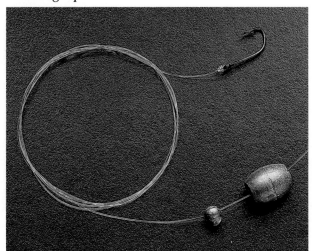

MAKE an easy-to-tie slip-sinker rig by threading an egg sinker onto the line, pinching on a small split shot about 2 feet up the line, then attaching a hook.

FLOAT your bait off bottom by threading on a small marshmallow so it rides just ahead of the hook. Or, hook your bait on a floating jig head.

Hooking, Playing & Landing Trout

The light lines and leaders used by most trout fishermen can easily result in a break-off, unless you know how to hook, play and land the fish properly.

Trout have comparatively soft mouths, so you do not have to set the hook hard. The fine-wire hooks on most flies and trout lures penetrate easily, assuming they're well-sharpened. Fly fishermen often make the mistake of jerking the rod too hard when a trout takes the fly, snapping the light tippet.

When you hook a trout, it usually makes a powerful initial run. Unless the fish heads for snaggy cover, don't try to stop it. With spinning tackle, make sure your drag is set on the light side. With a fly rod, let the reel handle spin freely; the clicker will prevent the line from overrunning. When you hook a large trout or salmon, it's a good idea to slow the run as soon as possible so the fish can't reach the rapids and swim into the next pool.

You may have to follow the fish if it takes too much line. After the initial run, start applying some pressure. Keep your rod tip high enough for the rod to absorb the force of a sudden run. If the fish jumps, quickly lower your rod tip to reduce the tension.

Otherwise, a head shake could break your line. Don't let the fish rest; it will soon tire if you maintain steady pressure.

Small trout hooked on a fly rod can be landed simply by stripping in line, but with bigger trout it pays to use your reel so you have the advantage of a mechanical drag.

If possible, fly fishermen should keep their entire leader outside the tip-top during the fight. The line-to-leader connection could hang up in the guides should a trout make a last-minute run, and the tippet could snap. Using a needle knot (p. 49) rather than a nail knot will minimize the problem.

When you plan on releasing the fish, play it as quickly as possible. If the fight drags on, the fish may become too stressed to survive. A light tippet, while considered very sporting, results in a longer fight that may kill the trout. Even if it swims away, it may die later.

Net the fish as shown on the following page, or beach it if you're near a gradually sloping bank. When you lead a trout into the shallows and it feels bottom, it often panics and beaches itself.

Tips for Hooking, Playing and Landing Trout on Flies

WAIT until the trout sucks in a dry fly and closes its mouth before setting the hook. If you try to set too soon, you'll pull the fly out of its mouth.

SET the hook by lifting the rod with a stiff wrist while stripping in line with your other hand. Lift the rod tip straight up rather than pulling back.

PALM the spool of an exposed-rim fly reel for extra drag. This keeps a big steelhead or salmon from getting into a rapids and running far downstream.

How to Net a Trout

KEEP your net out of the water while the trout is still "green." Putting the net into the water before the fish tires may cause it to dart away.

NET the trout headfirst when it tires, plunging the net under it quickly. To keep the fish from breaking off in the net, slacken the line as you lift.

AVOID chasing the trout with your net. If you attempt to net the trout tail-first, it may feel the net and surge forward, breaking your line.

Catch-and-Release

Production of trout can be measured like production of crops. Just as farmers record crop yields in bushels per acre, fisheries managers record trout yields in pounds per acre.

Hat Creek, a heavily fished California stream, produces about 60 pounds of trout per acre per year. In 1983, a creel census was conducted on a 3½-mile stretch of the stream which had a total annual production estimated at 2800 pounds of trout. In that year, fishermen caught over 20,000 pounds of trout, over 7 times the productive capacity of the stream. Fortunately, most of these fish were released. It's obvious that this stream could not continue to provide good fishing for the entire season, unless fishermen returned a good share of their trout to the water.

Heavy fishing pressure on some popular streams has prompted conservation agencies to install catch-and-release regulations. And even where such regulations are not in effect, more and more fishermen are voluntarily returning most of their trout.

There's no disputing the concept of catch-and-release fishing, but unless fishermen know exactly how to release their fish, many will die from mishandling. If you follow the procedure shown at right, the trout and salmon you release will have an excellent chance of survival.

FLATTEN your barbs so hooks can be removed without injuring the fish. By keeping a tight line during the fight, you will seldom lose a fish.

MOVE to a location out of the current to play the fish. This way, it cannot use the current to its advantage, so it tires more quickly.

LEAVE the fish in the water, grasp the hook with a pliers or hemostat, then shake the hook to release the fish. This way, you won't remove the protective slime.

CUT the leader if a fish is deeply hooked. In a Wisconsin study, 56 percent of deep-hooked trout survived when the leader was cut; 11 percent when the hook was removed.

HOLD the fish in an upright position facing into the current. Give it time to recover so it can swim away on its own. If it starts to sink, hold it upright a while longer.

AVOID landing salmon with a tailer. When the noose tightens around the tail, scales are removed, making the fish susceptible to infection.

High Water

To trout fishermen, high water can be a blessing or a curse. Runoff from a heavy rain or rapid snowmelt raises the stream level and discolors the water, but the effects of these changes depend upon the type of stream and your method of fishing.

Anadromous trout and salmon are drawn into streams by the rising water. But fishing may be tough as long as the water stays muddy; as it starts to clear, the action picks up dramatically. Fishing peaks when the water is clearing, but still somewhat discolored.

Resident trout become much less wary in discolored water, and more likely to stray from cover. They feed more actively because of the food washed in by the runoff. So you do not have to present your bait as precisely as you normally would.

But even though the trout are feeding, fishing is more difficult in high water because the current is swifter and the water deeper, making it hard to get your lure or bait deep enough.

Spinfishermen can get deep simply by using more weight, but it's not as easy for fly fishermen. Split-shot, lead-core line, shooting heads and large weighted nymphs and streamers all help to solve the problem. But trout still have difficulty spotting a fly.

Lures that produce vibration, like spinners and plugs, are more effective in discolored water. Trout detect the vibrations with their lateral-line sense. Bright colors also help. Fly materials like Flashabou®, Krystal Flash™ and tinsel improve the visibility of streamers and large wet flies. In extremely muddy water, natural bait is the best choice. Trout can smell the bait, even when they can't see it.

Streams vary in the amount of time necessary for the water to clear and return to normal level. It may take two weeks in a stream with a large drainage area, but only a few days in one with a small drainage. In tailwater streams (p. 37), the water may rise and fall daily. Experienced fishermen know which streams in their area clear soonest, and plan their fishing accordingly.

Generally, headwaters clear first. If the lower reaches of a stream are too muddy for fly fishing, you may find water that's clear enough by hiking upstream. Sometimes you only have to go far enough to get above a muddy tributary.

FLOAT-FISH in high water to minimize the effects of the current. As you float, cast a crankbait to the bank, then start reeling immediately so the plug dives. With the boat

Lures for High Water

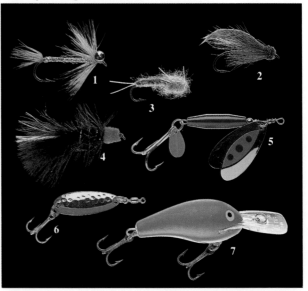

POPULAR LURES include: (1) Comet, a lead-eye fly that sinks fast; (2) Krystal Flash Muddler, for extra visibility; (3) George's Brown Stone Nymph (weighted); (4) Flash-A-Bugger, also highly visible; (5) Bolo® spinner; (6) Krocodile® spoon; (7) Fat Rap®.

floating at the speed of the current, drag is eliminated and the plug can get deep enough to catch bank-hugging trout. Some anglers throw a drag chain out the bow to slow the drift slightly and keep the boat floating parallel to shore. Floating may be the only effective method in streams where high water makes wading too treacherous.

Tips for Fishing in High Water

CAST upstream with a spinner, spoon or plug; retrieve within inches of the bank. Trout hold tight to the bank because the current is slower and the water often clearer.

SPLICE 2 feet of lead-core line to your leader butt to get your fly deep. Nail-knot or snell (p. 102) a foot of 20-pound mono to each end of the lead-core. Tie loops (p. 68) at the ends.

TIE a bucktail streamer upside down on the hook so the wing covers the point. The fly will ride with the point up, so you can fish deep in fast current without snagging.

Low Water

When the water is low and the stream shrinks to a fraction of its former size, all the trout concentrate in a few key spots, usually the deepest pools, runs

and undercuts. Consequently, you can find the trout much more easily than in high water. But low water also means clear water, so the fish are spookier and more selective.

Practically all trout streams have low water at some time of year. Freestone streams have low-water problems more often than limestone streams because they lack the spring-water flow that provides a stabilizing influence on water levels. When there is little precipitation or snowmelt, the water level drops and the clarity increases.

With the water so transparent, it's easier to walk along the stream and spot the trout, but they can also see you more clearly. Because the low water

LURES include drab-colored flies like (1) Arbona Wiggle Nymph, (2) Light Cahill Thorax, (3) Parachute Adams, (4) Extended Green Drake, and (5) Black Ant; (6) Tiger Tail™; (7) Teeny Wee-Crawfish™; (8) marabou jig.

How to Avoid Spooking Low-Water Trout

SIDE-CAST to keep your rod and line low. Otherwise, trout could easily see them glinting in the sunlight through the crystal-clear water. The problem is greatest in fly casting, because the rod is so long and the line so thick. If your rod were held high for a normal overhead cast, it would be directly in the trout's line of sight. By holding the rod and line low, you keep them under the line of sight, outside the window of vision.

leaves them fewer places to hide and thus more visible to predators, they become much warier.

When trout become super-selective, fly fishermen gain an edge over anglers using other methods. Not only does a fly have a natural look, but it allows a presentation more delicate than possible with other lures and baits. In low, clear water, fly fishermen use rods of 5-weight or lighter, leaders as long as 15 feet, and tippets as light as 6X.

Flies for low water are smaller than normal, usually size 16 or under, with drab, natural colors. Dries and nymphs generally work better than streamers. Terrestrial patterns, like a black ant, are a good choice when nothing is rising. Low-water periods usually correspond to the times when terrestrial insects are most numerous.

How you approach trout is important under any conditions, but the importance increases when the water is low and clear. Step lightly, keep a low profile, and wear drab clothing. You may have to crawl along the streambank to spot the trout, then plan your approach to avoid throwing a shadow over the lie.

Low-water fishing is usually best in overcast or windy weather; trout cannot see you as well as they could under calm, sunny conditions. Trout are most active in early morning, around dusk, or at night. In midday, they tuck into heavy cover or move to deep water and feed very little.

Heavy Cover

If you watched fisheries workers electrofishing a small trout stream, you'd be amazed at the number of trout living in dense brush piles, weedbeds and log jams, or far beneath undercut banks and overhanging limbs.

Stream trout are conditioned to seek heavy cover at an early age. Soon after they emerge from the redd, they face attacks from predatory insects, birds and fish, including larger trout. Those that learn to find the cover that affords the greatest protection have the best chance of survival.

Many anglers do not even attempt to fish these prime spots, for fear of getting snagged. There is no escaping the fact that snags are going to be a problem, but if you want to catch these wary trout, which usually are the biggest trout, you must learn to fish heavy cover.

By learning to side-cast with a fly rod, for instance, you can place a fly beneath overhanging branches. A side cast is just like a conventional cast, except that the rod is held parallel to the water. With a little practice, you can cast beneath cover only a few inches off the water, precisely controlling your distance.

Fly fishing also works well for fishing undercut banks. You can often drift a fly beneath a bank that could not be reached with other lures or bait (photos at right).

Trout tucked in dense weedbeds are difficult to catch on spinning lures because weeds quickly foul the hooks. But you can easily float a dry fly over the weed tops, or fish a sinking fly in pockets or channels in the weeds. With fly tackle you can cast across a weedbed to open water, retrieve the fly to the edge of the weeds, then pick it up for another cast without dragging it back through them.

Jigs work well for drawing trout out of heavy cover. Cast as close to a log jam, brushpile or undercut as you can; a jig sinks fast enough to reach the fish zone before the current carries it away. With spinning gear and a brushguard jig, you can keep snagging to a minimum.

You can also draw trout from heavy cover with a spinner or small spoon. Position yourself upstream, cast down to the cover, then hang the lure in the current along the upstream edge and sides. If lures fail to pull trout from the cover, try natural bait. Pinch on a split-shot 6 to 12 inches from a plain hook, add a worm or salmon egg, then drift the bait past the lie.

When you hook a trout, try to get it away from the cover immediately. If you let it run, it will invariably head for the thickest tangle of weeds or brush.

With any of these heavy-cover techniques, it pays to use heavier-than-normal line and tippets, preferably abrasion-resistant mono. Soft mono scuffs too easily and could cost you a good trout.

SPECIAL LURES AND FLIES for heavy cover include (1) Dave's Hopper, a floating grasshopper imitation; (2) Marabou Muddler with wings tied below the hook to reduce snagging; (3) Whitlock Chamois Leech with mono weedguard; (4) Coho, a streamer tied upside-down for fewer snags; (5) Nature Jig®; (6) Canyon weedless jig; (7) Weedless Triple Ripple Stump Jumper®; (8) Super Vibrax®; (9) K-O Wobbler®.

How to Fly-Fish an Undercut

QUARTER your cast upstream so your fly, usually a terrestrial, nymph or wet, alights close to the bank and several feet upstream of the undercut.

ALLOW the fly to drift freely; if the current is angling into the bank, it will pull the fly beneath the overhang where trout can easily see it.

Tips for Fishing Heavy Cover

FLICK a sidearm cast under overhanging brush. Raise the rod slightly on the backcast so the line won't slap the water behind you; lower it as the line unrolls to the rear, then make a forward cast just above the water.

UNSNAG a fly by raising your rod tip, then throwing a loop as if making a roll cast (p. 72). When the loop unrolls on the opposite side of the snag, the fly will usually pull free.

Night Fishing

CLIP a light to your vest for selecting flies or lures, tying knots, untangling lines and leaders, and unhooking fish. A gooseneck model leaves your hands free.

To many, the notion of fishing a trout stream at night evokes thoughts of tripping over logs and tangling lines in streamside brush. But to others, night fishing means big trout, especially browns.

Big browns stay in heavy cover during daylight hours, but at night they seem to lose their caution. They feed in shallow riffles and tails of pools, often far from cover, and are not nearly as selective as in daylight. Cutthroat and rainbows also feed at night, but to a lesser extent.

Night fishing is most effective during low-water periods in summer, when the clarity increases because of the low flow and the water temperature may rise into the 70s. At night, the water may cool to the mid-60s, a more likely temperature for feeding, and the clarity is actually an advantage. Moonless, starry nights are best; trout are less wary in the dark of the moon, but the stars provide enough light so you can see a little.

Before attempting to fish at night, scout the water during the day. Remember likely trout lies, overhead branches or other obstacles that could foul your cast, deep holes that you could step into while wading, and gradually sloping banks where you could easily land a good-sized trout. Nighttime is not the time to check out new water.

Fly fishermen most commonly use streamers, nymphs or leech imitations, usually in large sizes. During a major hatch, you can often hear trout rising. In this situation, dry flies can be very effective. Many night fishermen prefer big, heavily hackled dry flies because they are easier to see and produce plenty of vibrations so trout can quickly locate them. A light-colored fly is also easier to see, and at night the exact color is not as important as the silhouette.

After dark, spinfishermen catch a lot of big browns by casting minnow plugs, spinners or small spoons into a riffle, then reeling them rapidly downstream. Live bait is usually fished in slower water; a gob of worms, a whole crawler, or a chub tail is a good choice.

Because the fish are more aggressive at night, your presentation need not be as delicate as in daylight. In fact, a fly splatting down on the water may actually attract a trout's attention. You can get by with a 6- to 8-pound spinning line or fly tippet, so if you do get snagged in streamside brush you can pull loose. A heavy tippet will also straighten out better on the cast.

You don't need a lot of special equipment for night fishing, but unless you're very familiar with the streambed, it's a good idea to wear waders instead of hip boots. Bug spray, a flashlight, and a light that attaches to your vest also come in handy.

POPULAR LURES for night fishing include (1) Black Filoplume Leech; (2) Simulator; (3) Troth Bullhead; (4) Hexagenia; all large, highly visible flies; (5) Floating Rapala®; (6) Teeny-R®; a rattling crankbait; (7) Cyclone; and (8) Panther Martin®, a sonic spinner.

Tips for Night Fishing

ATTACH your fly with a tiny metal clip. This way, you do not have to tie knots in the dark.

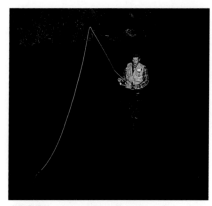

SPOOL on white fly line for night fishing. Any light-colored line will be visible, but white shows up best.

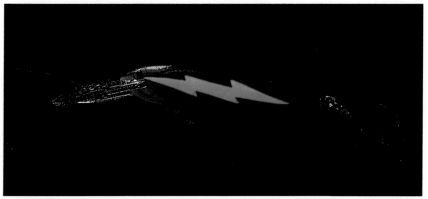

DOCTOR plugs, spinners and spoons with luminescent tape to improve lure visibility when night fishing. But do not use tape that glows too brightly; it will spook the fish. You can also buy luminescent fly-tying materials.

Winter Fishing

If you dislike crowds, try fishing your favorite trout stream in winter. Chances are you'll have the whole stream to yourself, and the trout can be surprisingly cooperative.

Of course, you should check the fishing regulations to make sure the stream is open. Many streams close before the fall spawning season and don't reopen until spring, and those that remain open often have special regulations, such as artificials-only or catch-and-release.

Most winter fishing is for browns, rainbows, cut-throat and brook trout, but anglers on Pacific-coast streams catch good numbers of winter-run steel-head. These fish enter the streams in late fall in preparation for spring spawning.

Trout behave much differently in near-freezing water than at summertime temperatures. Look for them in slower water and heavier cover. In most cases they're right on the bottom, although they will rise to feed on tiny emerging midges, or *snowflies*. Bright sunlight triggers these midge hatches, prompting trout to start feeding. Fly fishing with midge pupa patterns in sizes 18 to 28 can be very effective, especially on warm, sunny afternoons.

Many anglers think that flies this small must be difficult to use, so they shy away from midge fishing. But you can fish midges much the same way you

fish nymphs, only with lighter gear. Most midge fishermen use a 2- to 4-weight fly rod from 8 to 9 feet long. Midges work best when fished just beneath the surface film, so a floating, weight-forward fly line is a good choice. Use a 9- to 12-foot knotless leader with a 6x to 8x tippet. Strikes on midges are often very subtle, so it pays to attach a sensitive strike indicator.

Dry flies are seldom used in winter, but streamers, nymphs and scud patterns account for a fair number of trout. Streamers should be worked deep and slow. Nymphs and scuds should be dead-drifted, just as in summer.

Where live-bait fishing is legal, it works exceptionally well during the winter months. Western anglers catch lots of good-sized brown trout on sculpins. But small baits like waxworms, maggots, mayfly

and stonefly nymphs, salmon eggs and hellgrammites are the best choice for most stream trout fishing. Simply attach a small split-shot, and drift the morsel through a likely spot.

Steelhead anglers drift-fish with spawn bags or spawn imitations. The fish hold in slower water than they would in summer, and do not feed as aggressively. You have to drift the bait close to them, often dozens of times, to tempt a strike.

As a general rule, the best winter trout fishing is where the stream is warmest. Trout often congregate around springs because the ground water is normally warmer than the surrounding water. In some tailwater streams, trout stay in the vicinity of the dam because water discharged from the depths of the upstream reservoir is a few degrees warmer than water farther downstream.

Tips for Fishing a Midge

CHECK snowy streambanks to determine if there is a midge hatch. Tiny dark insects resembling mosquitos are probably midges; select a fly that resembles them.

DEAD-DRIFT a midge imitation just beneath the surface film, rather than on the surface. Your tippet will be less visible and the sunken fly seems to have more appeal.

REMOVE a midge from a trout's jaw with a hemostat. Because midges are so small, it takes too much time to remove them with your fingers. The stress caused by excess handling makes it difficult to release the trout alive.

Fishing for Trophy Trout

An average stream fisherman seldom catches a big trout. It's not that the big ones aren't there; anglers occasionally see them following lures or hear them taking insects on the surface. As proof that big trout exist, fisheries workers regularly take them with shockers during stream surveys, even on streams that are fished heavily.

The trophy fisherman catches considerably fewer trout, but the challenge of outwitting a big one makes up for the lack of quantity. To improve his chances of taking a trophy, he fishes in different places and uses different techniques than other anglers.

Look for big trout in the deepest pools or undercuts, or at least in areas where they can easily reach the deep-water retreat. Just how deep is relative; in a

small creek, a 4-foot pool is deep enough to hold a big one. In a large river, an 8-foot pool may not be deep enough.

Big trout prey on smaller ones, so when a likely-looking pool fails to produce even a small trout, this may be a clue that the pool is home to an exceptionally large trout. It pays to try such a pool from time to time rather than giving up on it.

Of course, some streams are more likely to produce big trout than others. Tailwater streams, coastal streams, and streams connected to large lakes generally yield the biggest trout. Some of the very best streams in these categories are identified in the following chapter.

A trophy trout is more likely to be near bottom than a small one, so sinking flies or deep-running lures are usually more effective than dry flies or shallow-runners.

Because fish make up a greater percentage of a trout's diet as it grows older, fish-imitating lures like minnow plugs, spinners and streamers take larger trout than small, insect-imitating flies. Some trophy hunters use 5-inch minnow plugs, or streamers that measure up to 4 inches.

Trout that have lived in a stream for many years and seen almost every possible lure are difficult to fool with even the most realistic artificial. But these old-timers can often be duped with live bait, preferably

HARD-TO-REACH pockets, like a deep hole beneath roots or branches, often hold big trout. Most anglers shy away from such spots because of snags.

DOWNSTREAM reaches that would seem too warm and muddy for trout usually have high baitfish populations that attract trophy browns.

REMOTE stream stretches or those where brushy banks restrict access usually hold bigger trout than easily accessible stretches.

a natural food captured in the stream. Western anglers, for instance, know that big browns have a weakness for sculpins, small fish that spend most of their time hiding under rocks. Other good baits for big trout include salmon eggs, chub tails, crayfish, waterworms, hellgrammites and nightcrawlers.

Big dry flies can be deadly during a hatch of large insects. In the northern Rockies, trophy-class trout that normally ignore insects go on a feeding rampage when large stoneflies, known as salmon flies, are hatching. On many eastern streams, big trout gorge themselves during the green drake mayfly hatch.

A hefty trout does not like to exert itself too much. Rather than racing smaller trout to catch fast-moving foods, it lies in wait for the chance to grab unsuspecting prey. Regardless of the type of bait or lure, a slow presentation generally works best.

Any type of trout fishing requires an inconspicuous approach to avoid putting the fish down. But when you're after trophies, stealth is even more important. The reason these trout have grown so large is that they have learned to sense predators, including fishermen. If they detect any unusual movement or vibration, they immediately head for cover and refuse to bite. Some trophy specialists go to extremes to avoid detection; they cast from behind bushes, or stay upstream of the pool and let the current carry their bait to the fish. For trophy browns, serious anglers do almost all their fishing at night.

POPULAR LURES for trophy fishing include (1) Olive Wool-Head Sculpin, (2) Muddler Minnow, (3) weighted Bitch Creek Nymph, (4) Extended Green Drake, (5) Elk Hair Salmon, (6) Dahlberg Diver, (7) Mouserat, (8) Dave's Crayfish, (9) Comet, (10) Diving Bang-O-Lure.

Blue-Ribbon Trout Streams

Finding a good place to fish is one of the biggest problems facing the average stream-trout angler. In most regions of the country, prime trout water is at a premium, and local anglers are not too generous when it comes to volunteering information on their favorite stream.

If you try contacting state or provincial natural-resources agencies to find a productive fishing spot, you may be disappointed with the information they provide. These agencies often avoid advertising their prime trout streams for fear of attracting too many anglers and causing trout populations to be overfished.

You can find some information in trout magazines, but chances are you won't find anything on the region you're interested in fishing.

To help fishermen make their choice, Hunting and Fishing Library researchers spent months gathering information on the continent's best trout and salmon streams. Information came from knowledgeable anglers, guides, biologists, game wardens, outdoor writers, members of our own staff, and anyone else who had fished or studied a lot of trout streams.

The information presented here includes not only the names of the best streams, but the types of water, the most productive reaches and the major trout or salmon species present.

Eastern Streams

In North America, the sport of fly fishing for trout was born on eastern streams. Even today, streams like the Beaver Kill are synonymous with quality fly fishing.

Despite extremely heavy fishing pressure, especially around population centers, eastern streams continue to provide good trout fishing. Many of the heavily fished streams must be stocked to meet the demand, but there are plenty of streams in remote areas with good populations of wild brook and brown trout. In fact,

improving water quality in recent years has added to the number of trout-stream miles.

Most eastern trout streams are of the freestone variety. While these streams usually have good populations of trout, especially brookies, the fish sometimes run on the small side. Limestone streams are much less common but hold considerably larger trout, particularly browns. The better limestone streams typically produce numbers of 12- to 15-inchers, with an occasional 4- to 6-pounder. Fishing Creek, a limestone stream in Pennsylvania, produced a 15-pound, 4-ounce brown trout in 1977.

Fly fishing on most eastern streams is best from April through June, the time of heaviest insect hatches. Hardware and bait fishing stays good all year.

The biggest eastern trout come from tailwater streams. Most are stocked with rainbows and browns, and commonly produce trophies from 8 to 10 pounds. The Smith River in Virginia, which drains Philpott Reservoir, yielded an 18-pound, 11-ounce brown in 1979. Although tailwater streams generally lack nat-

ural reproduction, they are quite fertile and have a long growing season because their water stays fairly warm during the winter. The warmer water also means that trout will start to bite earlier in the season than on most other streams. And in summer the water stays cool, so trout continue to bite.

The East's best fishing for brook trout is found in Maine, with some quality streams in Vermont and New Hampshire. If you want big brookies, 12- to 15-inchers, look for a good-sized stream off the beaten track. The larger fish are quickly removed on heavily fished streams. Brook trout generally bite best from April through June on large streams, April through July on smaller ones.

Many lakes in the northern part of the region support populations of good-sized brook trout, brown trout, rainbow trout and landlocked salmon. These species enter connecting streams in spring and fall for feeding and spawning, and offer excellent fishing opportunities. Spring fishing is best from April through June; fall fishing in September and October.

For those interested in quantity of trout more than size, mountain streams are the best bet. National forest lands throughout the East are laced with thousands of miles of small, out-of-the-way trout streams that produce plenty of 6- to 8-inch brookies. In the southern part of the region, mountain streams are the only ones cold enough to support trout. Fishing in most mountain streams starts picking up in March or April and stays good through the summer.

Eastern streams are not without their problems. Acid rain has affected trout fishing in some parts of the East, especially the Adirondacks. When streams acidify, brown trout are the first to disappear. Brook trout are more acid-tolerant and can persist longer, but even they have vanished from some streams.

Excessive fishing pressure has prompted special regulations on many eastern streams. Some streams have a no-kill regulation, meaning that all trout must be released. Others have trophy regulations, limiting anglers to one fish of specified trophy size. Other common regulations are fly-fishing only or artificial lures only.

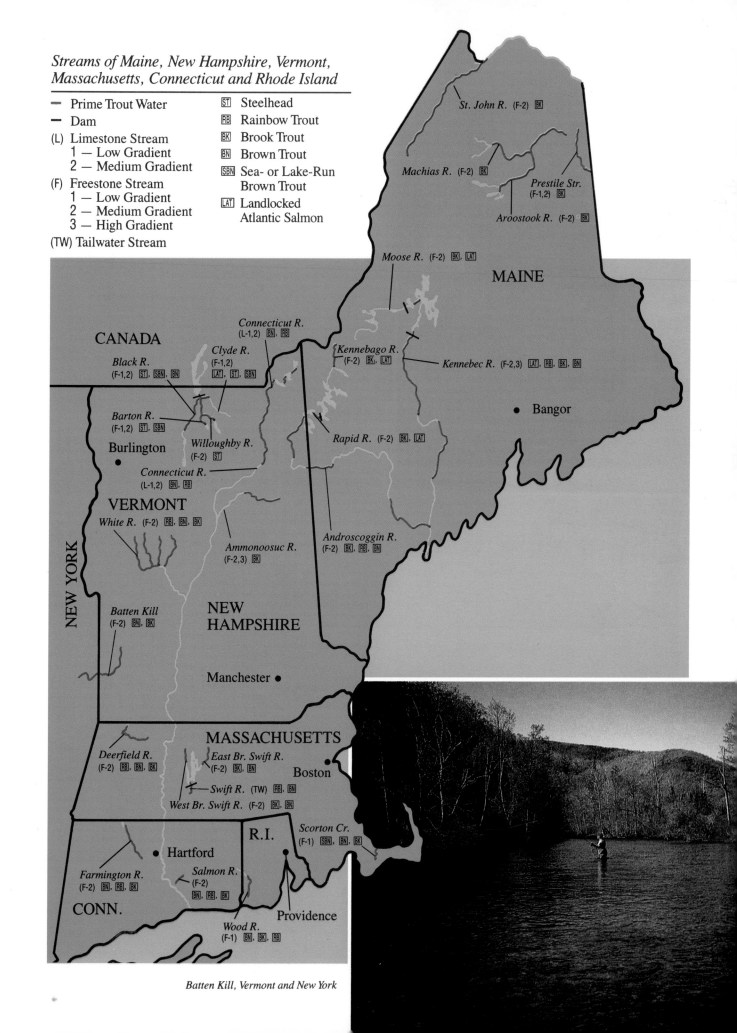

Streams of Maine, New Hampshire, Vermont, Massachusetts, Connecticut and Rhode Island

- — Prime Trout Water
- ▬ Dam
- (L) Limestone Stream
  - 1 — Low Gradient
  - 2 — Medium Gradient
- (F) Freestone Stream
  - 1 — Low Gradient
  - 2 — Medium Gradient
  - 3 — High Gradient
- (TW) Tailwater Stream

ST Steelhead
RB Rainbow Trout
BK Brook Trout
BN Brown Trout
SBN Sea- or Lake-Run Brown Trout
LAT Landlocked Atlantic Salmon

St. John R. (F-2) BK

Machias R. (F-2) BK

Prestile Str. (F-1,2) BK

Aroostook R. (F-2) BK

MAINE

Moose R. (F-2) BK, LAT

CANADA

Connecticut R. (L-1,2) BN, RB

Clyde R. (F-1,2) LAT, ST, SBN

Kennebago R. (F-2) BK, LAT

Kennebec R. (F-2,3) LAT, RB, BK, BN

Black R. (F-1,2) ST, SBN, BN

Barton R. (F-1,2) ST, SBN

Willoughby R. (F-2) ST

Burlington

Bangor

Rapid R. (F-2) BK, LAT

Connecticut R. (L-1,2) BN, RB

VERMONT

White R. (F-2) RB, BN, BK

Ammonoosuc R. (F-2,3) BK

Androscoggin R. (F-2) BK, RB, BN

NEW YORK

Batten Kill (F-2) BN, BK

NEW HAMPSHIRE

Manchester ●

MASSACHUSETTS

Deerfield R. (F-2) RB, BN, BK

East Br. Swift R. (F-2) BK, BN

Boston ●

Swift R. (TW) RB, BN

West Br. Swift R. (F-2) BK, BN

R.I.

Scorton Cr. (F-1) SBN, BK

Hartford ●

Salmon R. (F-2) BN, RB, BK

Farmington R. (F-2) BN, RB, BK

Providence

CONN.

Wood R. (F-1) BN, BK, RB

Batten Kill, Vermont and New York

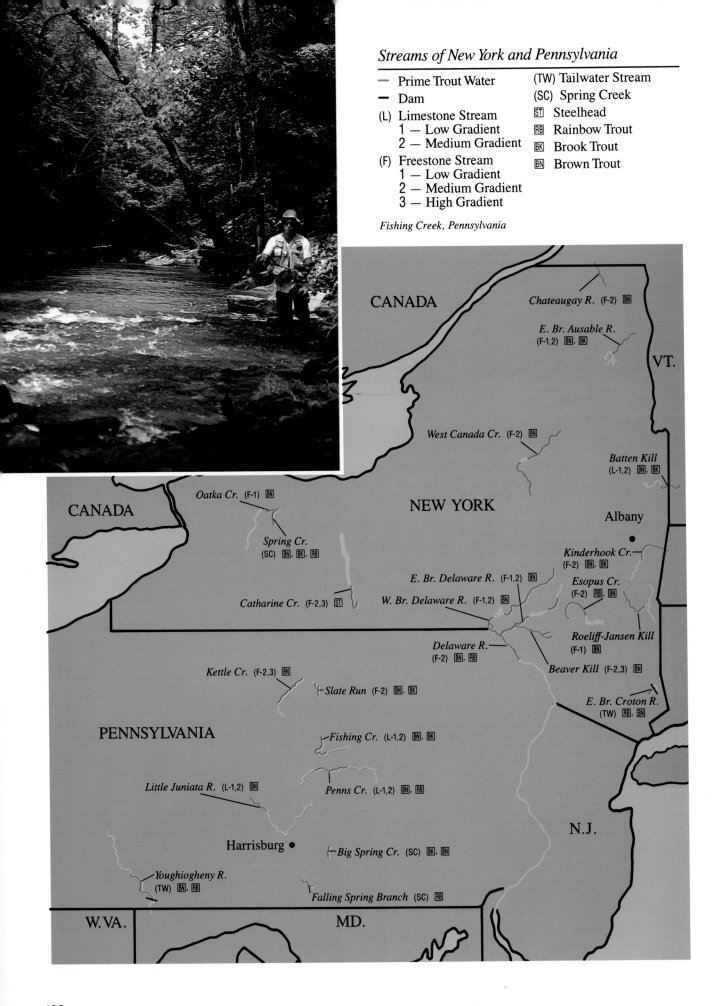

Streams of New York and Pennsylvania

— Prime Trout Water
– Dam
(L) Limestone Stream
　1 — Low Gradient
　2 — Medium Gradient
(F) Freestone Stream
　1 — Low Gradient
　2 — Medium Gradient
　3 — High Gradient

(TW) Tailwater Stream
(SC) Spring Creek
ST Steelhead
RB Rainbow Trout
BK Brook Trout
BN Brown Trout

Fishing Creek, Pennsylvania

CANADA

CANADA

NEW YORK

VT.

Albany

Harrisburg ●

PENNSYLVANIA

N.J.

W. VA.

MD.

Chateaugay R. (F-2) BN

E. Br. Ausable R. (F-1,2) BN, BK

West Canada Cr. (F-2) BN

Batten Kill (L-1,2) BN, BK

Oatka Cr. (F-1) BN

Spring Cr. (SC) BN, BK, RB

Catharine Cr. (F-2,3) ST

E. Br. Delaware R. (F-1,2) BN

W. Br. Delaware R. (F-1,2) BN

Kinderhook Cr. (F-2) BN, BK

Esopus Cr. (F-2) RB, BN

Delaware R. (F-2) BN, RB

Roeliff-Jansen Kill (F-1) BN

Kettle Cr. (F-2,3) BN

Slate Run (F-2) BN, BK

Beaver Kill (F-2,3) BN

E. Br. Croton R. (TW) RB, BN

Fishing Cr. (L-1,2) BN, BK

Little Juniata R. (L-1,2) BN

Penns Cr. (L-1,2) BN, RB

Big Spring Cr. (SC) BK, BN

Youghiogheny R. (TW) BN, RB

Falling Spring Branch (SC) RB

132

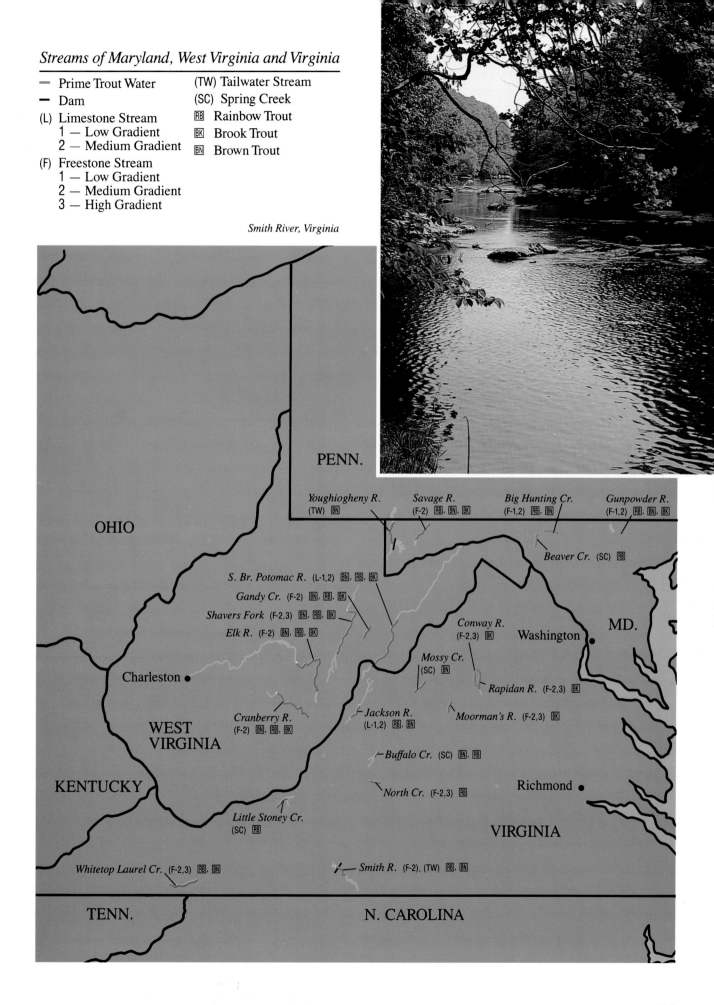

Streams of Maryland, West Virginia and Virginia

– Prime Trout Water
– Dam
(L) Limestone Stream
1 — Low Gradient
2 — Medium Gradient
(F) Freestone Stream
1 — Low Gradient
2 — Medium Gradient
3 — High Gradient

(TW) Tailwater Stream
(SC) Spring Creek
RB Rainbow Trout
BK Brook Trout
BN Brown Trout

Smith River, Virginia

PENN.

OHIO

Youghiogheny R. (TW) BN

Savage R. (F-2) RB, BN, BK

Big Hunting Cr. (F-1,2) RB, BN

Gunpowder R. (F-1,2) RB, BN, BK

Beaver Cr. (SC) RB

S. Br. Potomac R. (L-1,2) BN, RB, BK

Gandy Cr. (F-2) BN, RB, BK

Shavers Fork (F-2,3) BN, RB, BK

Elk R. (F-2) BN, RB, BK

Conway R. (F-2,3) BK

Washington

MD.

Charleston

Mossy Cr. (SC) BN

Rapidan R. (F-2,3) BK

WEST VIRGINIA

Cranberry R. (F-2) BN, RB, BK

Jackson R. (L-1,2) RB, BN

Moorman's R. (F-2,3) BK

KENTUCKY

Buffalo Cr. (SC) BN, RB

Richmond

North Cr. (F-2,3) RB

Little Stoney Cr. (SC) RB

VIRGINIA

Whitetop Laurel Cr. (F-2,3) RB, BN

Smith R. (F-2), (TW) RB, BN

TENN.

N. CAROLINA

133

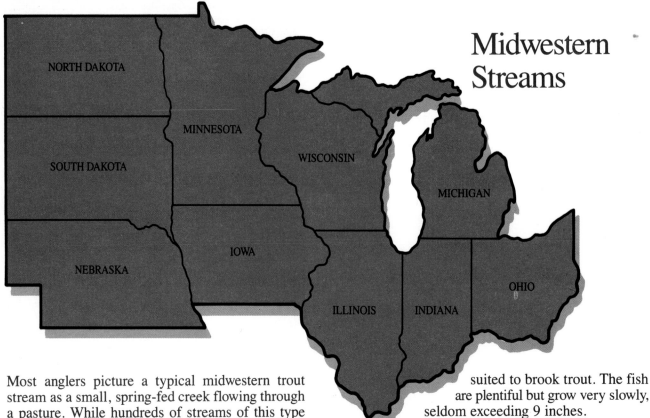

Midwestern Streams

Most anglers picture a typical midwestern trout stream as a small, spring-fed creek flowing through a pasture. While hundreds of streams of this type are scattered through the Midwest, there are many other types of streams as well, including some of the country's finest trout water.

In the Dakotas, tailwater zones below Missouri River dams produce dozens of trophy browns and rainbows each season. The Garrison tailrace in North Dakota yielded a 23-pound, 4-ounce brown in 1982 and a 20-pound, 4-ounce rainbow in 1984.

The Black Hills are laced with lightly fished trout streams that are very similar to quality streams in the West, but smaller in size. The main stems of these streams offer good fishing for browns and rainbows, the headwaters for brook trout.

Streams in the northern part of Michigan's lower peninsula grow much bigger brookies. In these larger, more fertile waters, the fish top out at about 17 inches. In many of these streams, good-sized browns are found in the lower sections, where the water is warmer.

The streams of southeastern Minnesota, southwestern Wisconsin and northeastern Iowa offer good fishing for a variety of trout. Many of these fertile streams flow through steep-sided limestone ravines and have ample supplies of spring water. Browns, the most common species, occasionally reach weights over 10 pounds. Some of the streams are cold enough for brook trout, and a few support rainbows.

In the northern part of the region are numerous small, infertile streams flowing over beds of granite. These streams have very cold water and are best suited to brook trout. The fish are plentiful but grow very slowly, seldom exceeding 9 inches.

The most famous midwestern streams, like Wisconsin's Brule and Michigan's AuSable, are included in the section on Great Lakes tributaries (p. 148).

Fishing in midwestern streams is usually best in spring and early summer, when streams are starting to warm, and in fall, when they start to cool. In summer, aquatic vegetation in streambeds sometimes makes fishing difficult. Heavy brush or tall weeds along the bank can also be a problem. In most streams, seasons close before the fall spawning period, but a few remain open all winter.

Midwestern streams are plagued by a variety of problems ranging from overgrazing to flash flooding. When cattle are allowed to graze too close to the streambank, they eat the vegetation that would keep the banks from eroding in high water. When the banks collapse, the streambed silts over, covering the gravel that produces insects and provides spawning habitat.

Flash flooding results mainly from excessive drainage of agricultural lands. With fewer lakes, ponds and marshes to hold water, runoff flows directly into the streams, eroding the banks, creating massive log jams, and sometimes shifting portions of the channel.

Another common problem is beaver damage. Although beaver dams may create productive pools on high-gradient streams, they cause major problems on streams with lower gradient. They block spawning migrations, and the ponds that form above the dams have warm water and silty bottoms.

Streams of North Dakota, South Dakota and Nebraska

- **━** Prime Trout Water
- **▬** Dam
- (F) Freestone Stream
  - 1 — Low Gradient
  - 2 — Medium Gradient
  - 3 — High Gradient
- (TW) Tailwater Stream
- RB Rainbow Trout
- BN Brown Trout
- BK Brook Trout

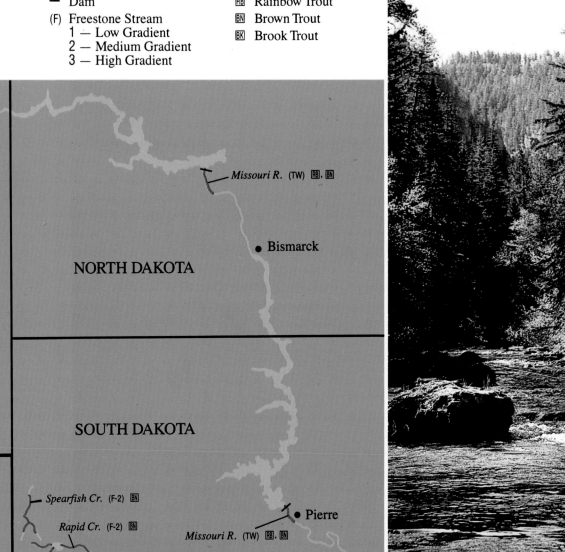

Missouri R. (TW) RB, BN

● Bismarck

NORTH DAKOTA

SOUTH DAKOTA

Spearfish Cr. (F-2) BN

Rapid Cr. (F-2) BN

Missouri R. (TW) RB, BN

● Pierre

Castle Cr. (F-2,3) BN, RB, BK

Soldiers Cr. (F-1,2) BN

Long Pine Cr. (F-1,2) RB, BN

White R. (F-1) BN

Snake R. (TW) RB, BN

N. Br. Verdigre Cr. (F-1) RB

North Platte R.

NEBRASKA

Sutherland Canal (TW) RB
(Nebraska Public Power District
(NPPD) Supply Canal)

North Platte

Spearfish Creek, South Dakota

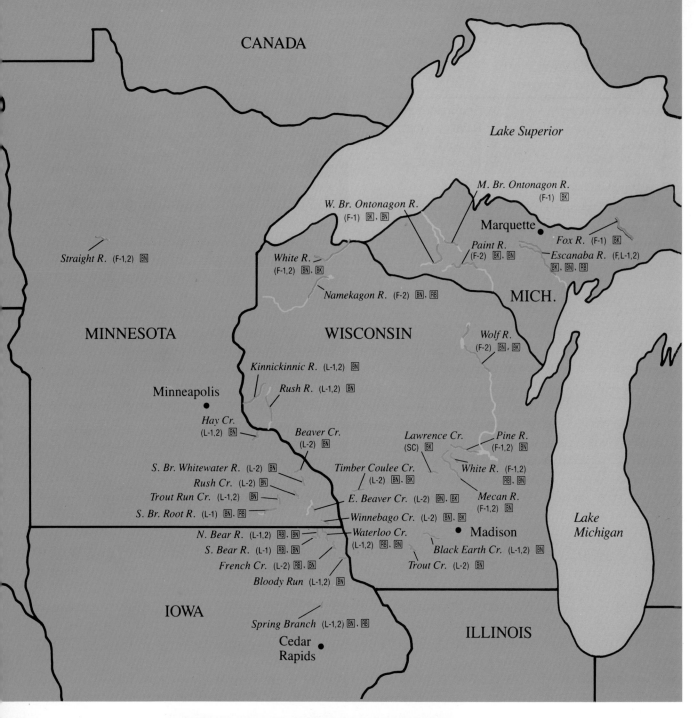

CANADA

Lake Superior

M. Br. Ontonagon R.
(F-1) BK

W. Br. Ontonagon R.
(F-1) BK , BN

Marquette •

Fox R. (F-1) BK

Paint R.
(F-2) BK , BN

Escanaba R. (F,L-1,2)
BK , BN , RB

Straight R. (F-1,2) BN

White R.
(F-1,2) BN , BK

MICH.

MINNESOTA

Namekagon R. (F-2) BN , RB

WISCONSIN

Wolf R.
(F-2) BN , BK

Kinnickinnic R. (L-1,2) BN

Rush R. (L-1,2) BN

Minneapolis •

Hay Cr.
(L-1,2) BN

Beaver Cr.
(L-2)

Lawrence Cr.
(SC) BK

Pine R.
(F-1,2) BN

S. Br. Whitewater R. (L-2) BN

Timber Coulee Cr.
(L-2) BN , BK

White R. (F-1,2)
RB , BN

Rush Cr. (L-2) BN

Trout Run Cr. (L-1,2) BN

Mecan R.
(F-1,2) BN

S. Br. Root R. (L-1) BN , RB

E. Beaver Cr. (L-2) BN , BK

Winnebago Cr. (L-2) BN , BK

N. Bear R. (L-1,2) RB , BN

Waterloo Cr.
(L-1,2) RB , BN

• Madison

S. Bear R. (L-1) RB , BN

Black Earth Cr. (L-1,2) BN

French Cr. (L-2) RB , BN

Trout Cr. (L-2) BN

Lake Michigan

Bloody Run (L-1,2) BN

IOWA

Spring Branch (L-1,2) BN , RB

ILLINOIS

Cedar •
Rapids

Streams of Minnesota, Wisconsin, Michigan U.P. and Iowa

— Prime Trout Water
(L) Limestone Stream
   1 — Low Gradient
   2 — Medium Gradient
(F) Freestone Stream
   1 — Low Gradient
   2 — Medium Gradient
   3 — High Gradient
(SC) Spring Creek
RB Rainbow Trout
BN Brown Trout
BK Brook Trout

Trout Run Creek, Minnesota

AuSable River, Michigan

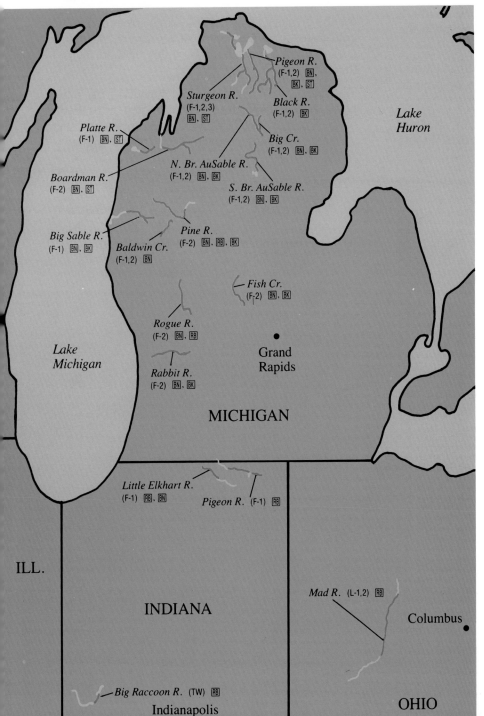

Streams of Michigan, Ohio and Indiana

— Prime Trout Water
— Dam
(L) Limestone Stream
    1 — Low Gradient
    2 — Medium Gradient
(F) Freestone Stream
    1 — Low Gradient
    2 — Medium Gradient
    3 — High Gradient
(TW) Tailwater Stream
RB Rainbow Trout
BN Brown Trout
BT Brook Trout
ST Steelhead

*Note: Great Lakes
tributary streams
are shown on pages
148-151.*

Southern Streams

Trout fishing in the South doesn't get much press, but this region has a surprising number of good streams, including some that produce trout of world-record proportions.

Most southern streams, particularly those in the Deep South, are much too warm for trout. But streams with an ample supply of cold water from springs or cold-water draws often support healthy trout populations, as do streams at high altitudes, where the air is considerably cooler. Many of the best southern trout streams have a heavy overstory to shade the water and keep it cool.

Fluctuating water levels and siltation limit natural reproduction in most southern streams, so populations must be maintained by stocking.

The biggest trout come from tailwater streams, especially those where baitfish rather than insects

are the primary forage. These large streams, fed by cold water from the depths of reservoirs, may stay cold enough for trout for 50 miles or more below the dam.

Tailwater streams are stocked heavily with rainbows, but intense fishing pressure often crops them off before they reach trophy size. Nevertheless, the streams commonly produce 2- to 5-pound rainbows

White River, Arkansas

Streams of Missouri, Arkansas and Oklahoma

— Prime Trout Water	(TW) Tailwater Stream
▬ Dam	(SC) Spring Creek
(L) Limestone Stream	RB Rainbow Trout
1 — Low Gradient	BN Brown Trout
2 — Medium Gradient	CT Cutthroat Trout

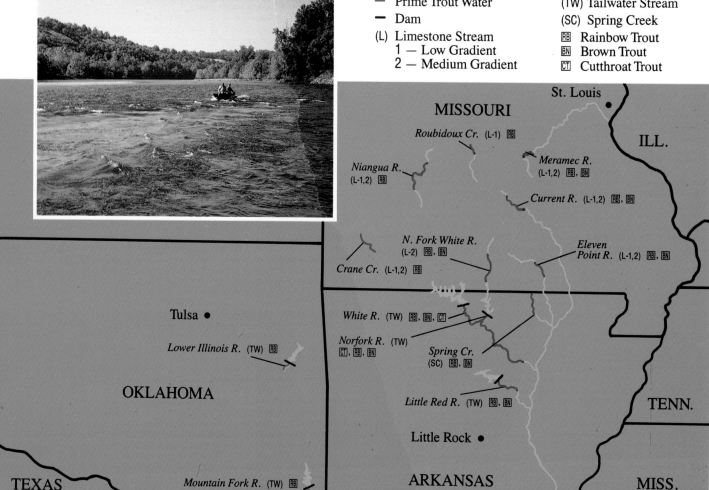

with an occasional 10- to 15-pounder. Brown trout, being more difficult to catch, have greater trophy potential. A 33-pound, 8-ounce brown was caught in the White River, Arkansas, below the Bull Shoals Dam, in 1977. Cutthroat trout have been stocked in some tailwater streams and are showing a lot of promise, with fish up to 9 pounds reported three years after stocking.

Fishing on most tailwater streams is best from late winter to midsummer. Downstream reaches of many tailwater streams become too warm for trout in late summer because not enough cold water is discharged from the dam. Grocery baits are popular for freshly stocked trout, and minnow plugs account for a good share of the trophies.

Low- to medium-gradient limestone streams in Tennessee, the Kentucky Bluegrass region, and the Ozarks of Missouri and Arkansas also offer good trout fishing. Generally, these streams originate from large springs and flow through areas with a lot of exposed limestone rock.

A few of these streams support wild trout populations, but most are managed on a put-and-take or put-grow-and-take basis. Trout grow rapidly in the fertile water, but heavy fishing pressure removes most of them by the end of the season, before they have much chance to grow. Most run 10 to 14 inches, with carry-over fish reaching 18.

Mountain streams in the Appalachians often have native brook trout, particularly in the headwaters. In many mountain streams, rainbows and browns have been stocked and are reproducing. Although these streams are fed by small springs, most are infertile, so trout grow slowly. Brook trout average only about 6 inches, with a few reaching 12. Rainbows and browns run from 8 to 11 inches, with a few up to 14.

Spinfishing with natural bait, spinners and small minnow plugs is popular on both mountain streams and limestone streams, and there is a considerable amount of fly fishing on streams that aren't too overgrown. Fishing is best in early spring and late fall. Trout are active then, and fishing pressure is lighter.

The best mountain streams are those in state and national parks, some of which allow only catch-and-release fishing. Numerous mountain streams have been degraded by strip mining, and many Appalachian streams have been damaged by acid rain.

Wilson Creek, North Carolina

Streams of Kentucky, Tennessee, the Carolina's and Georgia

- — Prime Trout Water
- ▬ Dam
- (L) Limestone Stream
  - 1 — Low Gradient
  - 2 — Medium Gradient
- (F) Freestone Stream
  - 1 — Low Gradient
  - 2 — Medium Gradient
  - 3 — High Gradient
- (TW) Tailwater Stream
- BK Brook Trout
- RB Rainbow Trout
- BN Brown Trout

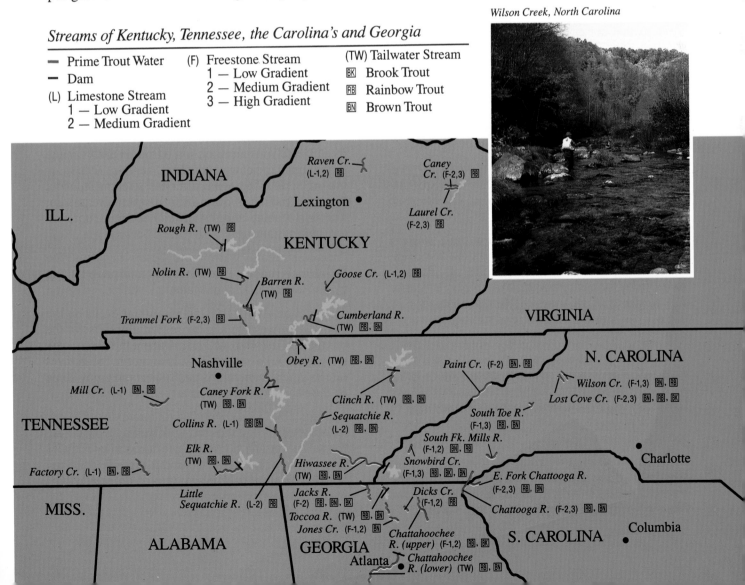

Western Streams

The West is famed for its premier stream-trout fishing, particularly in mountainous areas of Montana, Idaho and Wyoming. Steelhead and salmon abound in the coastal streams of Washington and Oregon (p. 152). This section in the book includes only the inland streams of the West. Here, the predominant species are rainbow, brown and cutthroat trout; but many other salmonids are caught, including brook trout, bull trout, Dolly Varden, grayling and golden trout.

Throughout the West, particularly in national forests and mountainous regions, are thousands of miles of trout streams that seldom see a fisherman. This water is inaccessible by road, but you can find outstanding fishing if you do a little hiking. These streams have good populations of native trout and require no stocking.

Streams that are easy to reach are heavily fished, so they must be carefully regulated. On certain streams, you must abide by slot limits; these require you to release trout within a specified size range. The Yellowstone River for a few miles below Yellowstone Lake is Wyoming's most popular trout stream, yet it produces an astounding number of 14- to 18-inch cutthroat because of a no-kill regulation.

In streams where cutthroat fishing is not strictly regulated, populations are quickly fished down. Cutthroat are easy to catch, and they do not compete well with other trout species.

Wading is the favorite way to fish most western streams. But some of the big rivers are too deep, and even if you could wade them, the best water is miles from the nearest road. So the only effective way to fish is by floating. McKenzie boats (p. 60), specially designed for this type of fishing, are a common sight on the big rivers.

Western streams are known for good-sized trout, especially the famous rivers in southwestern Montana like the Madison. These streams are cold yet fertile, so trout grow rapidly. Some have dozens of miles of prime trout water, and can absorb a lot of fishing pressure.

However, the biggest trout do not come from streams like the Madison, but from lakes and the rivers that feed and drain them. Tailwater streams, like the South Fork of the Snake River below Idaho's

Palisades Reservoir, yield a surprising number of trophy trout, including browns over 15 pounds.

Most western streams are fed by snowmelt from the mountains. You can catch some trout in early spring; but once the heavy snowmelt begins, fishing is tough. It picks up again after the streams subside. The best fishing is often in fall, when streams are low and stable, and fishermen become more interested in hunting.

Tailwater streams warm more slowly than those fed by surface runoff. Insect hatches and peak fishing times run about a month later.

The salmon-fly hatch is an important event on the calendar of western anglers, especially those in the vicinity of Yellowstone Park. During the hatch, usually in late June or early July, trout gorge themselves on the emerging nymphs and fishermen enjoy some of the year's fastest action.

Although the West abounds with quality trout water, many streams face serious problems. Dewatering for irrigation and domestic use sometimes reduces flow to the point where a stream actually dries up. Another common problem is erosion, caused by overgrazing of streambanks.

Streams of Interior Washington, Oregon, California and Nevada

- — Prime Trout Water
- ▬ Dam
- (F) Freestone Stream
  - 1 — Low Gradient
  - 2 — Medium Gradient
  - 3 — High Gradient
- (TW) Tailwater Stream
- (SC) Spring Creek
- ST Steelhead Trout
- RB Rainbow Trout
- BN Brown Trout
- SBN Sea- or Lake-Run Brown Trout
- BK Brook Trout
- CT Cutthroat Trout
- DV Dolly Varden
- GN Golden Trout

Note: Pacific Coast streams are shown on pages 152-155.

WASHINGTON Spokane

MT.

Spokane R. (F-2) RB, BN, BK

Rocky Ford Cr. (SC) RB, BN

Yakima R. (F-1,2) RB, CT

Portland

Metolius R. (SC) RB, BN, BK, DV

Malheur R. (F-2) RB, DV

OREGON

IDAHO

Williamson R. (F-1) RB, ST, BK

Sprague R. (F-1,2) BN, RB, BK

Donner und Blitzen R. (F-3) RB

McCloud R. (F-2) RB, BN, SBN

Fall R. (F-1,2) RB, BN

Hat Cr. (F-1) RB, BN

NEVADA

Yellow Cr. (F-1) RB, BN

Truckee R. (F-1,2) RB, BN

CALIFORNIA

Sacramento

Reno

Mid. Fk. Stanislaus R. (F-3) RB, BN

E. Walker R. (F-2) RB, BN

Merced R. (F-1,3) RB, BN

Owens R. (F-1,2), (TW) BN, RB, SBN

Hot Cr. (SC) BN

Kings R. (F-1,3) BN, RB

S. Fk. Kern R. (F-2,3) RB, GN

Hat Creek, California

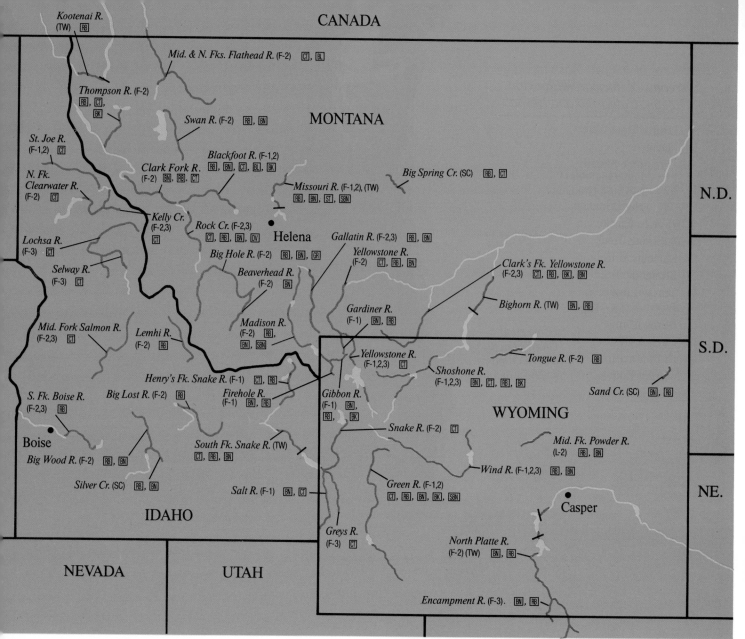

CANADA

MONTANA

Kootenai R.
(TW) RB

Mid. & N. Fks. Flathead R. (F-2) CT, BL

Thompson R. (F-2)
RB, CT, BK

Swan R. (F-2) RB, BN

St. Joe R.
(F-1,2) CT

Clark Fork R.
(F-2) BN, RB, CT

Blackfoot R. (F-1,2)
RB, BN, CT, BL, BK

Big Spring Cr. (SC) RB, CT

N.D.

N. Fk.
Clearwater R.
(F-2) CT

Kelly Cr.
(F-2,3)
CT

Rock Cr. (F-2,3)
CT, RB, BN, DV

Helena

Missouri R. (F-1,2), (TW)
RB, BN, ST, SBN

Lochsa R.
(F-3) CT

Big Hole R. (F-2) RB, BN, GR

Gallatin R. (F-2,3) RB, BN

Yellowstone R.
(F-2) CT, RB, BN

Clark's Fk. Yellowstone R.
(F-2,3) CT, RB, BK, BN

S.D.

Selway R.
(F-3) CT

Beaverhead R.
(F-2) BN

Gardiner R.
(F-1) BN, RB

Bighorn R. (TW) BN, RB

Mid. Fork Salmon R.
(F-2,3) CT

Lemhi R.
(F-2) RB

Madison R.
(F-2) RB,
BN, SBN

Yellowstone R.
(F-1,2,3) CT

Tongue R. (F-2) RB

Shoshone R.
(F-1,2,3) BN, CT, RB, BK

Sand Cr. (SC) BN, RB

Henry's Fk. Snake R. (F-1) CT, RB

Firehole R.
(F-1) RB, RB

Gibbon R.
(F-1) BN,
RB, BK

WYOMING

S. Fk. Boise R.
(F-2,3) RB

Big Lost R. (F-2) RB

Boise

Snake R. (F-2) CT

Mid. Fk. Powder R.
(L-2) RB, BN

Big Wood R. (F-2) RB, BN

South Fk. Snake R. (TW)
CT, RB, BN

Wind R. (F-1,2,3) RB, BN

Casper

NE.

Silver Cr. (SC) RB, BN

Salt R. (F-1) BN, CT

Green R. (F-1,2)
CT, RB, BN, BK, SBN

IDAHO

Greys R.
(F-3) CT

North Platte R.
(F-2) (TW) BN, RB

NEVADA

UTAH

Encampment R. (F-3). BN, RB

Streams of Montana, Idaho and Wyoming

— Prime Trout Water
— Dam
(L) Limestone Stream
   2 — Medium Gradient
(F) Freestone Stream
   1 — Low Gradient
   2 — Medium Gradient
   3 — High Gradient
(TW) Tailwater Stream
(SC) Spring Creek

ST Steelhead
RB Rainbow Trout
BN Brown Trout
SBN Sea- or Lake-Run
   Brown Trout
BK Brook Trout
CT Cutthroat Trout
BL Bull Trout
DV Dolly Varden
GR Grayling

Yellowstone River, Montana

Streams of Colorado, Utah, Arizona and New Mexico

- — Prime Trout Water
- ▬ Dam
- (F) Freestone Stream
  - 1 — Low Gradient
  - 2 — Medium Gradient
  - 3 — High Gradient
- (TW) Tailwater Stream
- RB Rainbow Trout
- BN Brown Trout
- SBN Sea- or Lake-Run Brown Trout
- BK Brook Trout
- CT Cutthroat Trout

South Platte River, Colorado

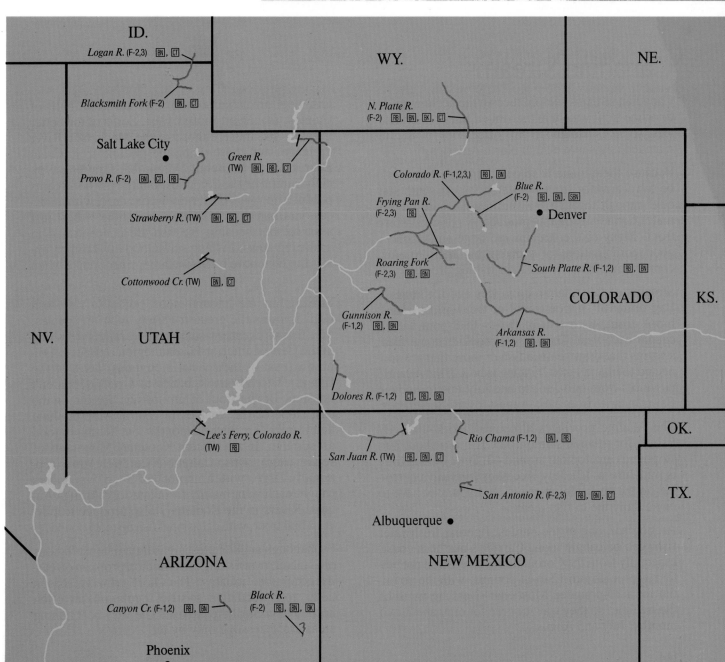

ID.

WY.

NE.

Logan R. (F-2,3) BN, CT

Blacksmith Fork (F-2) BN, CT

N. Platte R. (F-2) RB, BN, BK, CT

Salt Lake City ●

Green R. (TW) BN, RB, CT

Colorado R. (F-1,2,3,) RB, BN

Blue R. (F-2) RB, BN, SBN

Provo R. (F-2) BN, CT, RB

Frying Pan R. (F-2,3) RB

● Denver

Strawberry R. (TW) BN, BK, CT

Roaring Fork (F-2,3) RB, BN

South Platte R. (F-1,2) RB, BN

Cottonwood Cr. (TW) BN, CT

COLORADO

KS.

Gunnison R. (F-1,2) RB, BN

Arkansas R. (F-1,2) RB, BN

NV.

UTAH

Dolores R. (F-1,2) CT, RB, BN

OK.

Lee's Ferry, Colorado R. (TW) RB

Rio Chama (F-1,2) BN, RB

San Juan R. (TW) RB, BN, CT

San Antonio R. (F-2,3) RB, BN, CT

TX.

Albuquerque ●

ARIZONA

NEW MEXICO

Canyon Cr. (F-1,2) RB, BN

Black R. (F-2) RB, BN, BK

Phoenix
●

ALASKA
YUKON
NORTHWEST TERRITORIES
NEWFOUNDLAND
LABRADOR
BRITISH COLUMBIA
ALBERTA
SASK.
MANITOBA
QUEBEC
ONTARIO
NOVA SCOTIA
NEW BRUNSWICK

Canadian Streams

Canadian streams seldom receive the acclaim given to prime trout waters in the United States. Nonetheless, some Canadian streams offer trout fishing unmatched anywhere else in North America.

Because the climate is so cold, streams that would be too warm for trout if located farther south stay cold enough through the summer. Despite the climate, Canadian streams produce lots of good-sized trout. Many of the streams are large and fertile, a good combination for growing big fish. Another contributing factor is the light fishing pressure.

Streams of the Atlantic provinces and the Hudson Bay drainage support some of the world's largest brook trout, with fish in the 6- to 8-pound class caught each year. The biggest brookies come from streams that draw sea-run fish or those that are connected to inland lakes. Fishing is best in the Atlantic provinces from mid-June to late July, and in Hudson Bay tributaries from early August to mid-September.

The Atlantic provinces also boast world-class fly fishing for Atlantic salmon. The fish run about 8 to 12 pounds and top out around 40. Peak fishing time is mid-June to late July. Access is carefully controlled on the best salmon rivers, and you may have to pay a daily fee to fish them.

Arctic char, one of the hardest-fighting freshwater fish, can be caught along Canada's northern coast, especially from the Coronation Gulf east. In the better rivers, char run 12 to 14 pounds, with the potential for a 30-pounder. Most char rivers are north of the treeline, so they stay ice-free for only about two months, July and August.

Grayling are common in the northern half of Canada, from Hudson Bay west. Some of the better grayling streams are those of the Mackenzie River drainage, and those along the treeline from Great Bear Lake to Churchill, Manitoba. Grayling typically run from 1 to 2 pounds, but the prime streams produce numbers of 2½- to 3-pounders, with an occasional fish up to 5. Grayling fishing is best just after ice-out because the fish are concentrated in spawning areas. Fishing stays good all summer, unless the fish move back to a larger river or lake when spawning has been completed.

Streams in the mountainous region of western Canada offer the greatest variety of trout species. You'll find excellent summertime rainbow fishing in the Central Interior Plateau region of British Columbia, east of the coastal mountains. Most of the fish run 1 to 3 pounds, but 5- to 8-pounders aren't unusual. Brown trout of similar size abound on the east slope of the Rockies in central Alberta. June and October are the best months, but fishing is good all summer. In the eastern Kootenay Mountains of southeastern British Columbia, cutthroat run exceptionally large, with a number of 3- to 5-pounders caught each year, mainly from late July through August. Rivers in the Kootenays also produce trophy-class bull trout, with occasional fish up to 25 pounds.

Even though angling pressure is light in most regions of Canada, overfishing is a common problem on easily accessible streams. The short growing season limits trout production, so strict regulations are often needed to control the harvest. The very best fishing areas are accessible only by air.

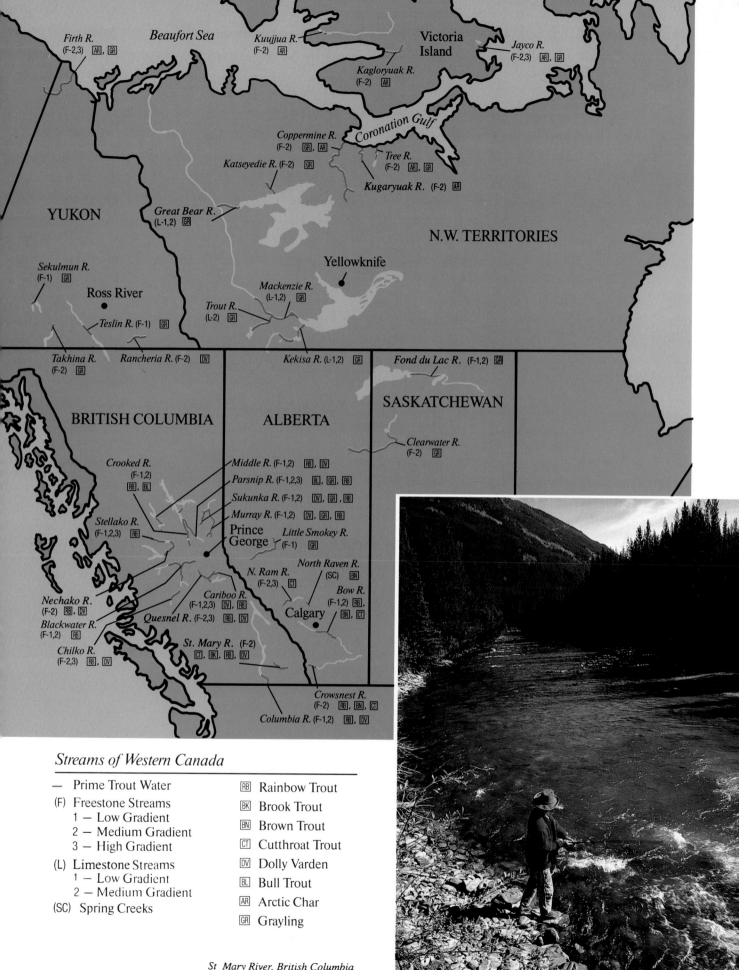

Firth R.
(F-2,3) [AR], [GR]

Beaufort Sea

Kuujjua R.
(F-2) [AR]

Victoria
Island

Jayco R.
(F-2,3) [AR], [GR]

Kagloryuak R.
(F-2) [AR]

Coronation Gulf

Coppermine R.
(F-2) [GR], [AR]

Tree R.
(F-2) [AR], [GR]

Katseyedie R. (F-2) [GR]

Kugaryuak R. (F-2) [AR]

YUKON

Great Bear R.
(L-1,2) [GR]

N.W. TERRITORIES

Sekulmun R.
(F-1) [GR]

Yellowknife

Ross River

Mackenzie R.
(L-1,2) [GR]

Teslin R. (F-1) [GR]

Trout R.
(L-2) [GR]

Takhina R.
(F-2) [GR]

Rancheria R. (F-2) [DV]

Kekisa R. (L-1,2) [GR]

Fond du Lac R. (F-1,2) [GR]

SASKATCHEWAN

BRITISH COLUMBIA

ALBERTA

Clearwater R.
(F-2) [GR]

Crooked R.
(F-1,2)
[RB], [BL]

Middle R. (F-1,2) [RB], [DV]

Parsnip R. (F-1,2,3) [BL], [GR], [RB]

Sukunka R. (F-1,2) [DV], [GR], [RB]

Murray R. (F-1,2) [DV], [GR], [RB]

Stellako R.
(F-1,2,3)
[RB]

Prince
George

Little Smokey R.
(F-1) [GR]

North Raven R.
(SC) [BN]

N. Ram R.
(F-2,3) [CT]

Bow R.
(F-1,2) [RB],
[BN], [CT]

Nechako R.
(F-2) [RB], [DV]

Cariboo R.
(F-1,2,3) [DV], [RB]

Blackwater R.
(F-1,2) [RB]

Quesnel R. (F-2,3) [RB], [DV]

Calgary

Chilko R.
(F-2,3) [RB], [DV]

St. Mary R. (F-2)
[CT], [BK], [RB], [DV]

Crowsnest R.
(F-2) [RB], [BN], [CT]

Columbia R. (F-1,2) [RB], [DV]

Streams of Western Canada

— Prime Trout Water

(F) Freestone Streams
   1 — Low Gradient
   2 — Medium Gradient
   3 — High Gradient

(L) Limestone Streams
   1 — Low Gradient
   2 — Medium Gradient

(SC) Spring Creeks

[RB] Rainbow Trout

[BK] Brook Trout

[BN] Brown Trout

[CT] Cutthroat Trout

[DV] Dolly Varden

[BL] Bull Trout

[AR] Arctic Char

[GR] Grayling

St Mary River, British Columbia

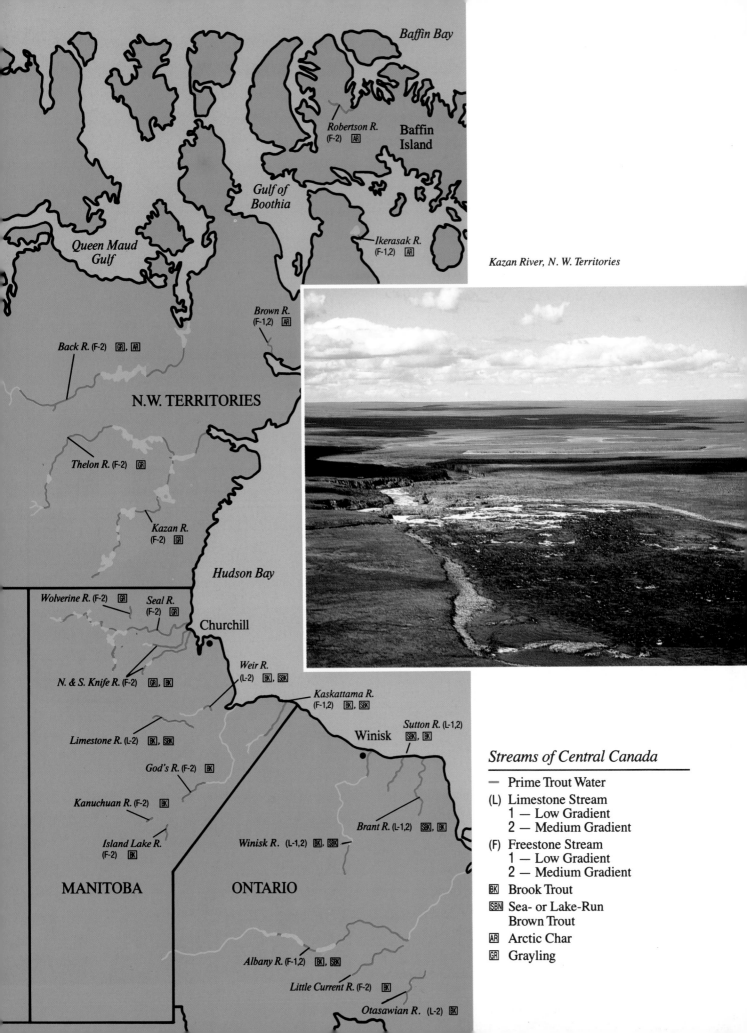

Baffin Bay

Robertson R.
(F-2) AR

**Baffin
Island**

*Gulf of
Boothia*

*Queen Maud
Gulf*

Ikerasak R.
(F-1,2) AR

Kazan River, N. W. Territories

Brown R.
(F-1,2) AR

Back R. (F-2) GR, AR

N.W. TERRITORIES

Thelon R. (F-2) GR

Kazan R.
(F-2) GR

Hudson Bay

Wolverine R. (F-2) GR   *Seal R.*
(F-2) GR

Churchill

Weir R.
(L-2) BK, SBK

N. & S. Knife R. (F-2) GR, BK

Kaskattama R.
(F-1,2) BK, SBK

Sutton R. (L-1,2)
SBK BK

Winisk

Limestone R. (L-2) BK, SBK

God's R. (F-2) BK

Brant R. (L-1,2) SBK BK

Kanuchuan R. (F-2) BK

Winisk R. (L-1,2) BK, SBK

Island Lake R.
(F-2) BK

MANITOBA   **ONTARIO**

Albany R. (F-1,2) BK, SBK

Little Current R. (F-2) BK

Otasawian R. (L-2) BK

Streams of Central Canada

— Prime Trout Water

(L) Limestone Stream
  1 — Low Gradient
  2 — Medium Gradient

(F) Freestone Stream
  1 — Low Gradient
  2 — Medium Gradient

BK Brook Trout

SBN Sea- or Lake-Run
     Brown Trout

AR Arctic Char

GR Grayling

Streams of Eastern Canada

- **—** Prime Trout Water
- **(L)** Limestone Stream
  - 2 — Medium Gradient
- **(F)** Freestone Stream
  - 1 — Low Gradient
  - 2 — Medium Gradient
  - 3 — High Gradient
- **BK** Brook Trout
- **SBK** Sea- or Lake-Run Brook Trout
- **SBN** Sea- or Lake-Run Brown Trout
- **AT** Atlantic Salmon
- **LAT** Land-locked Atlantic Salmon
- **AR** Arctic Char

Moisie River, Quebec

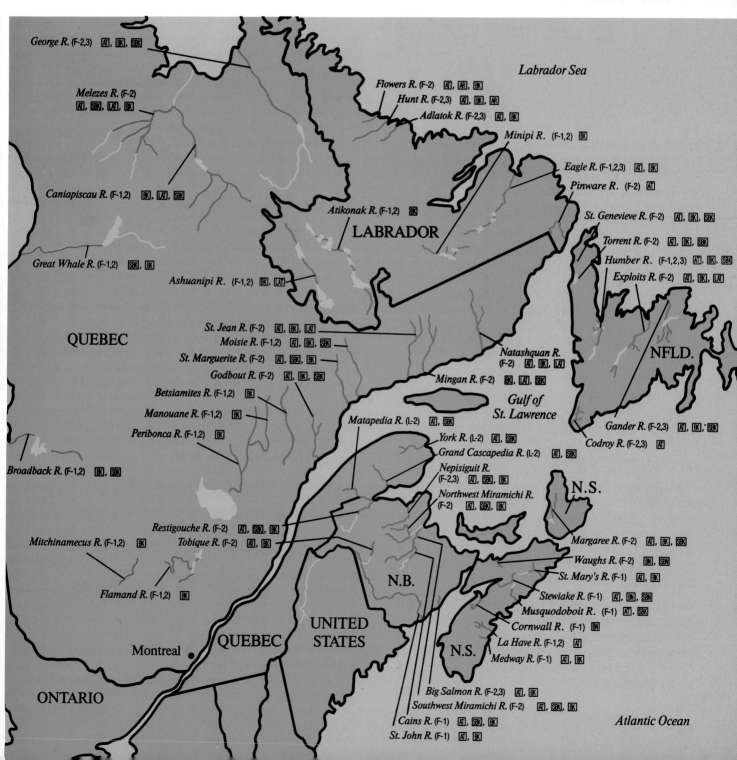

George R. (F-2,3) AT, BK, SBK

Melezes R. (F-2) AT, SBK, LAT, BK

Caniapiscau R. (F-1,2) BK, LAT, SBK

Great Whale R. (F-1,2) SBK, BK

Ashuanipi R. (F-1,2) BK, LAT

Flowers R. (F-2) AT, AR, BK

Hunt R. (F-2,3) AT, BK, AR

Adlatok R. (F-2,3) AT, BK

Minipi R. (F-1,2) BK

Atikonak R. (F-1,2) BK

LABRADOR

Labrador Sea

Eagle R. (F-1,2,3) AT, BK

Pinware R. (F-2) AT

St. Genevieve R. (F-2) AT, BK, SBK

Torrent R. (F-2) AT, BK, SBK

Humber R. (F-1,2,3) AT, BK, SBK

Exploits R. (F-2) AT, BK, LAT

NFLD.

QUEBEC

St. Jean R. (F-2) AT, BK, LAT

Moisie R. (F-1,2) AT, BK, SBK

St. Marguerite R. (F-2) AT, SBK, BK

Godbout R. (F-2) AT, BK, SBK

Betsiamites R. (F-1,2) BK

Manouane R. (F-1,2) BK

Peribonca R. (F-1,2) BK

Natashquan R. (F-2) AT, BK, LAT

Mingan R. (F-2) BK, LAT, SBK

Gulf of St. Lawrence

Gander R. (F-2,3) AT, BK, SBK

Codroy R. (F-2,3) AT

Broadback R. (F-1,2) BK, SBK

Matapedia R. (L-2) AT, SBK

York R. (L-2) AT, SBK

Grand Cascapedia R. (L-2) AT, SBK

Nepisiguit R. (F-2,3) AT, SBK, BK

Northwest Miramichi R. (F-2) AT, SBK, BK

N.S.

Mitchinamecus R. (F-1,2) BK

Restigouche R. (F-2) AT, SBK, BK

Tobique R. (F-2) AT, BK

Margaree R. (F-2) AT, BK, SBK

Waughs R. (F-2) BN, SBN

St. Mary's R. (F-1) AT, BK

Flamand R. (F-1,2) BK

N.B.

Stewiake R. (F-1) AT, BN, SBN

Musquodoboit R. (F-1) AT, SBK

UNITED STATES

QUEBEC

Cornwall R. (F-1) BN

N.S.

La Have R. (F-1,2) AT

Medway R. (F-1) AT, BK

Montreal

ONTARIO

Big Salmon R. (F-2,3) AT, BK

Southwest Miramichi R. (F-2) AT, SBK, BK

Cains R. (F-1) AT, SBK, BK

St. John R. (F-1) AT, BK

Atlantic Ocean

Great Lakes Tributaries

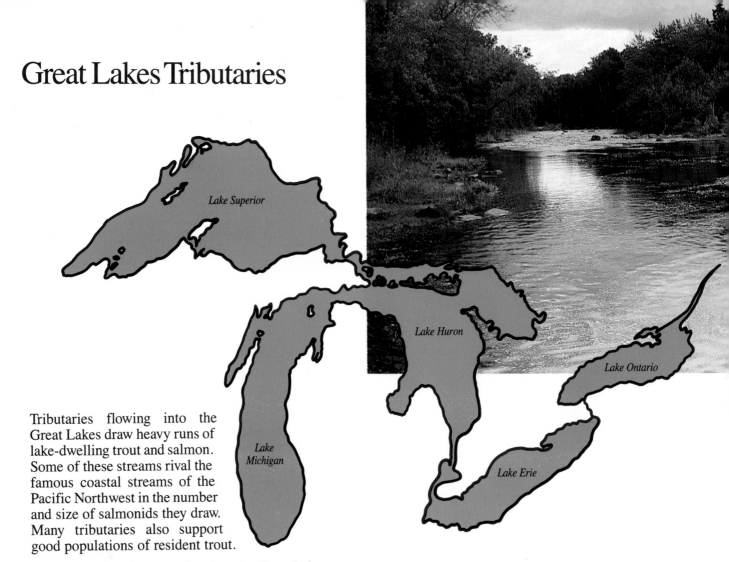

Lake Superior

Lake Huron

Lake Ontario

Lake Michigan

Lake Erie

Tributaries flowing into the Great Lakes draw heavy runs of lake-dwelling trout and salmon. Some of these streams rival the famous coastal streams of the Pacific Northwest in the number and size of salmonids they draw. Many tributaries also support good populations of resident trout.

A wide variety of streams flow into the Great Lakes, ranging from tiny creeks that completely stop flowing in dry periods to silty warmwater rivers large enough for seagoing vessels. Many of these streams do not fit into the usual stream categories, so classifications are not shown on the maps.

The best trout and salmon streams are spring-fed and have a relatively consistent flow; here, the fish reproduce naturally. In areas with good trout and salmon populations, almost all tributaries draw some spawners, though reproduction may not be successful.

Great Lakes tributaries are best known for their outstanding steelhead fishing. While the steelhead do not grow quite as large as those in coastal streams, 15-pounders are not unusual and 20- to 25-pounders are taken occasionally. The largest steelhead come from tributaries of Lake Ontario and from Canadian tributaries of Lake Huron.

Steelhead run in spring and again in fall. They spawn during the spring run; the fall run is a false run, meaning that no spawning takes place. Skamania steelhead, a summer-run strain that commonly reaches weights over 15 pounds, have been stocked in some Great Lakes tributaries.

The exact timing of the spring run depends on water temperature and stream flow. As a rule, the water must rise to 40°F before steelhead will start to enter the stream. Then, a heavy rain that causes stream levels to rise will draw large numbers of steelhead from the lake. Rain is also needed to trigger the fall run.

Besides steelhead, Great Lakes tributaries get good fall runs of coho, chinook and pink salmon. Some streams have good fall runs of brook or brown trout, and a few even draw lake trout.

On some tributaries, the summer or winter flow drops so low that a sandbar forms at the mouth. Fish cannot enter the stream until heavy runoff washes out the sandbar.

Many Great Lakes tributaries have some type of barrier, like a dam or waterfall, a short distance from the mouth. The barrier blocks the upstream movement of migratory salmonids. Only resident trout are found above it. Be sure you know the location of the barrier because fishing regulations above may differ from those below. Sometimes, natural-resources agencies install fish ladders or build step pools to allow migratory salmonids to reach upstream spawning areas.

Bois Brule River, Wisconsin

Lake Superior Tributaries

▬	Prime Trout Water	BN	Brown Trout
▬	Barrier to Upstream Migration	SBN	Sea- or Lake-Run Brown Trout
ST	Steelhead	PK	Pink Salmon
BK	Brook Trout	CO	Coho Salmon
SBK	Sea- or Lake-Run Brook Trout	CH	Chinook Salmon
		LT	Lake Trout

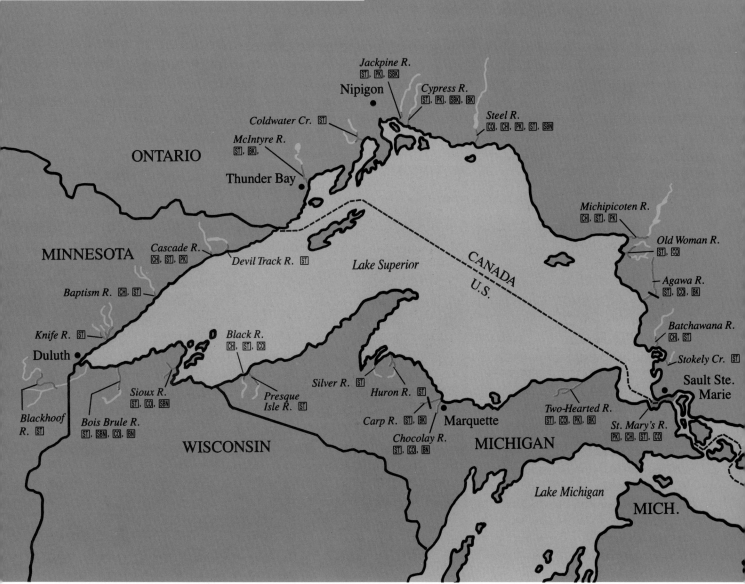

ONTARIO

Jackpine R.
ST, PK, SBK

Nipigon

Cypress R.
ST, PK, SBK, BK

Coldwater Cr. ST

McIntyre R.
ST, BK,

Thunder Bay

Steel R.
CO, CH, PK, ST, SBN

Michipicoten R.
CH, ST, PK

MINNESOTA

Cascade R.
CH, ST, PK

Devil Track R. ST

Lake Superior

CANADA
U.S.

Old Woman R.
ST, CO

Baptism R. CH, ST

Agawa R.
ST, CO, BK

Knife R. ST

Black R.
CH, ST, CO

Batchawana R.
CH, ST

Duluth

Silver R. ST

Sioux R.
ST, CO, SBN

Presque Isle R. ST

Huron R. ST

Stokely Cr. ST

Sault Ste. Marie

Blackhoof R. ST

Bois Brule R.
ST, SBN, CO, BN

Carp R. ST, BK

Chocolay R.
ST, CO, BN

Marquette

Two-Hearted R.
ST, CO, PK, BK

St. Mary's R.
PK, CH, ST, CO

WISCONSIN

MICHIGAN

Lake Michigan

MICH.

149

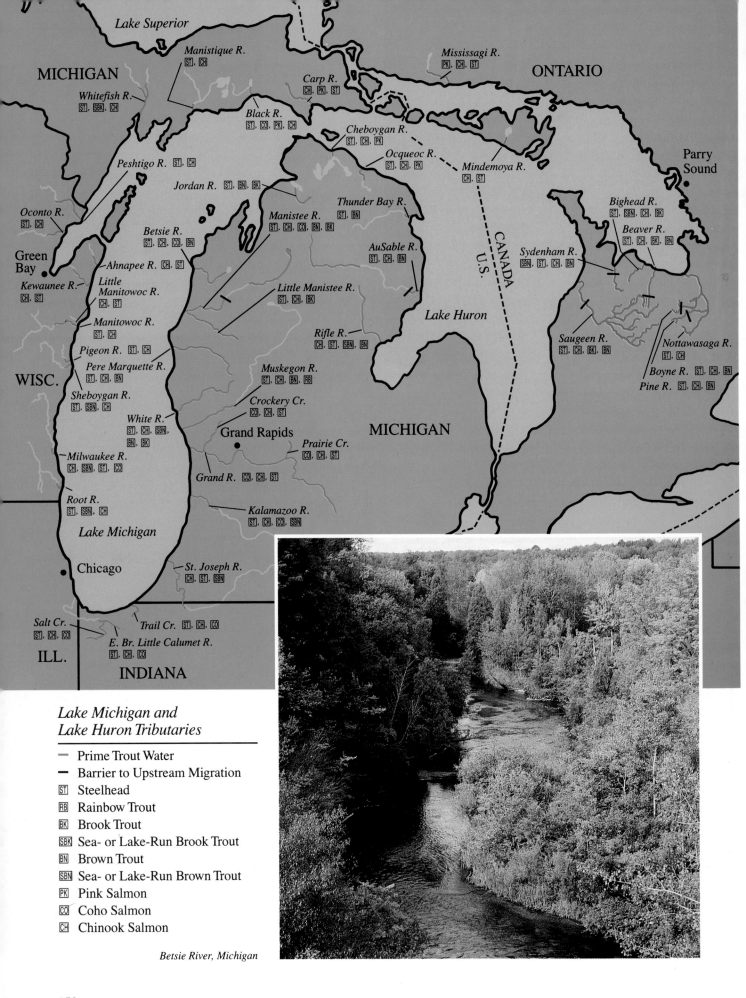

Lake Superior

MICHIGAN

Manistique R.
ST, CH

Whitefish R.
ST, SBK, CH

Carp R.
CH, PK, ST

Mississagi R.
PK, CH, ST

ONTARIO

Black R.
ST, CO, PK, CH

Cheboygan R.
ST, CH, PK

Ocqueoc R.
ST, CH, PK

Mindemoya R.
CH, ST

Parry Sound

Peshtigo R. ST, CH

Jordan R. ST, BN, BK

Thunder Bay R.
ST, BN

Oconto R.
ST, CH

Betsie R.
ST, CH, CO, BN

Manistee R.
ST, CH, CO, BN, BK

AuSable R.
ST, CH, BN

Bighead R.
ST, SBN, CH, BK

Beaver R.
ST, CH, BK, BN

Sydenham R.
SBN, ST, CH, BN

Green Bay

Ahnapee R. CH, ST

Little Manitowoc R.
CH, ST

Little Manistee R.
ST, CH, BK

Lake Huron

CANADA
U.S.

Kewaunee R.
CH, ST

Manitowoc R.
ST, CH

Rifle R.
CH, ST, SBN, BN

Saugeen R.
ST, CH, BK, BN

Nottawasaga R.
ST, CH

Pigeon R. ST, CH

Pere Marquette R.
ST, CH, BN

Muskegon R.
ST, CH, BN, RB

Boyne R. ST, CH, BN

Pine R. ST, CH, BN

WISC.

Sheboygan R.
ST, SBN, CH

Crockery Cr.
CO, CH, ST

White R.
ST, CH, SBN,
BN, BK

Grand Rapids

MICHIGAN

Milwaukee R.
CH, SBN, ST, CO

Prairie Cr.
CO, CH, ST

Grand R. CO, CH, ST

Root R.
ST, SBN, CH

Kalamazoo R.
ST, CH, CO, SBN

Lake Michigan

Chicago

St. Joseph R.
CH, ST, SBN

Salt Cr.
ST, CH, CO

Trail Cr. ST, CH, CO

E. Br. Little Calumet R.
ST, CH, CO

ILL.

INDIANA

Lake Michigan and Lake Huron Tributaries

— Prime Trout Water

— Barrier to Upstream Migration

ST Steelhead

RB Rainbow Trout

BK Brook Trout

SBK Sea- or Lake-Run Brook Trout

BN Brown Trout

SBN Sea- or Lake-Run Brown Trout

PK Pink Salmon

CO Coho Salmon

CH Chinook Salmon

Betsie River, Michigan

150

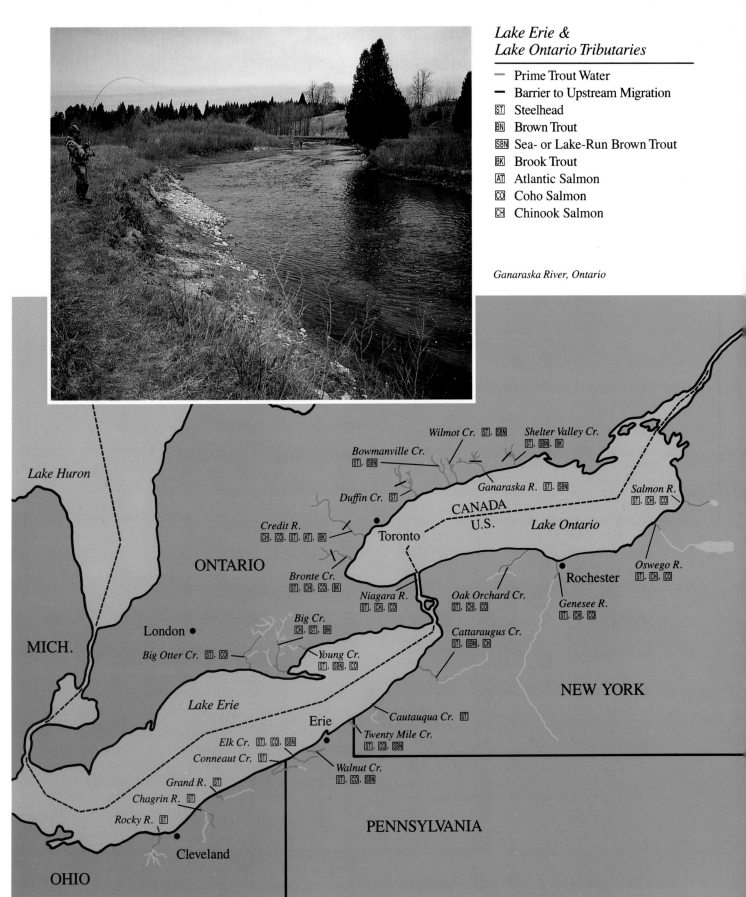

Lake Erie & Lake Ontario Tributaries

— Prime Trout Water
— Barrier to Upstream Migration
ST Steelhead
BN Brown Trout
SBN Sea- or Lake-Run Brown Trout
BK Brook Trout
AT Atlantic Salmon
CO Coho Salmon
CH Chinook Salmon

Ganaraska River, Ontario

Lake Huron

ONTARIO

Wilmot Cr. ST, SBN
Shelter Valley Cr. ST, SBN, BK
Bowmanville Cr. ST, SBN
Duffin Cr. ST
Ganaraska R. ST, SBN
Salmon R. ST, CH, CO

Credit R. CH, CO, ST, AT, BK
CANADA
U.S.
Lake Ontario

Toronto

Bronte Cr. ST, CH, CO, BK
Oswego R. ST, CH, CO

Niagara R. ST, CH, CO
Oak Orchard Cr. ST, CH, CO
Rochester
Genesee R. ST, CH, CO

MICH.

London ●
Big Cr. CH, ST, BN
Young Cr. ST, SBN, CO
Cattaraugus Cr. ST, SBN, CH

Big Otter Cr. ST, CO

NEW YORK

Lake Erie

Erie ●
Cautauqua Cr. ST
Twenty Mile Cr. ST, CO, SBN

Elk Cr. ST, CO, SBN
Conneaut Cr. ST
Walnut Cr. ST, CO, SBN
Grand R. ST
Chagrin R. ST
Rocky R. ST

PENNSYLVANIA

Cleveland

OHIO

Coastal Streams

Famed for their unparalleled Pacific salmon and steelhead fishing, the coastal streams of Oregon, Washington, British Columbia and Alaska attract anglers from across the continent. In addition to salmon and steelhead, many of these streams draw good runs of sea-run Dolly Varden and cutthroat trout. Numerous streams in Alaska and northern British Columbia also have excellent populations of resident rainbows and Arctic grayling.

The anadromous species get most of the attention because of their considerably larger size. Steelhead commonly run up to 20 pounds; the world record, weighing 42 pounds, 2 ounces, was taken at Bell Island, Alaska, in 1970. Chinook salmon frequently grow to 50 pounds; the world record, 97 pounds, 4 ounces, was caught in the Kenai River, Alaska, in 1985.

The timing of salmon runs varies considerably with latitude. The chinook run in Alaska starts about two months earlier than the run in Oregon. But the sequence of spawning runs of different species remains the same. Steelhead move into the streams in early spring, followed in order by chinooks, sockeyes, pinks and chums, then cohos and fall-run steelhead.

Alaskan runs are shorter in duration than those farther south because of the colder climate. Thus, the fish are more concentrated, resulting in excellent fishing. The best streams for variety, size and numbers of fish are found in southwest Alaska.

Runs of the same species take place at different times in different streams. Runs begin earlier in streams where the fish have to swim great distances to reach their spawning grounds.

Summer-run steelhead, for instance, may enter a stream in July, then swim hundreds of miles upstream before spawning the following March. Winter-run steelhead may move into a shorter stream in February, running upstream only a fraction of the distance before spawning a month later. A few streams have both summer- and winter-run fish.

Rainfall and tides have a great influence on steelhead and salmon runs. Increased flow from a heavy rain draws the fish into the stream. Fishing is best when the water starts to clear. The fish also ride in on high tides.

In some rivers, trout and salmon swim hundreds of miles upstream to reach their spawning grounds; the very best fishing, especially in Alaska and British

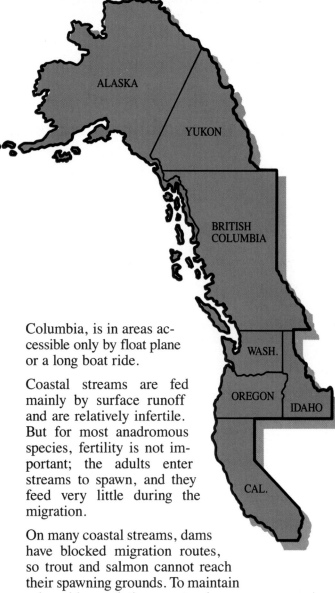

Columbia, is in areas accessible only by float plane or a long boat ride.

Coastal streams are fed mainly by surface runoff and are relatively infertile. But for most anadromous species, fertility is not important; the adults enter streams to spawn, and they feed very little during the migration.

On many coastal streams, dams have blocked migration routes, so trout and salmon cannot reach their spawning grounds. To maintain salmonid populations, natural-resources agencies must stock these streams.

Dams also create another problem: the plunging water becomes supersaturated with nitrogen. The blood of fish below the dam absorbs too much nitrogen, causing gas-bubble disease, which may be fatal. This problem has been corrected on most streams by redesigning the dams to eliminate plunging water. Other threats to salmonid populations include commercial fishing and Indian netting.

Fishing for resident rainbows peaks in fall; grayling are easily caught throughout the season. Practically all resident trout follow the spawning salmon, feeding heavily on their eggs. After the salmon leave, the resident fish disperse, becoming more difficult to find.

The sport-fishing season on most coastal streams is continuous, although some streams or sections of them are closed for a time to insure that enough fish reach the spawning grounds to produce a satisfactory year-class.

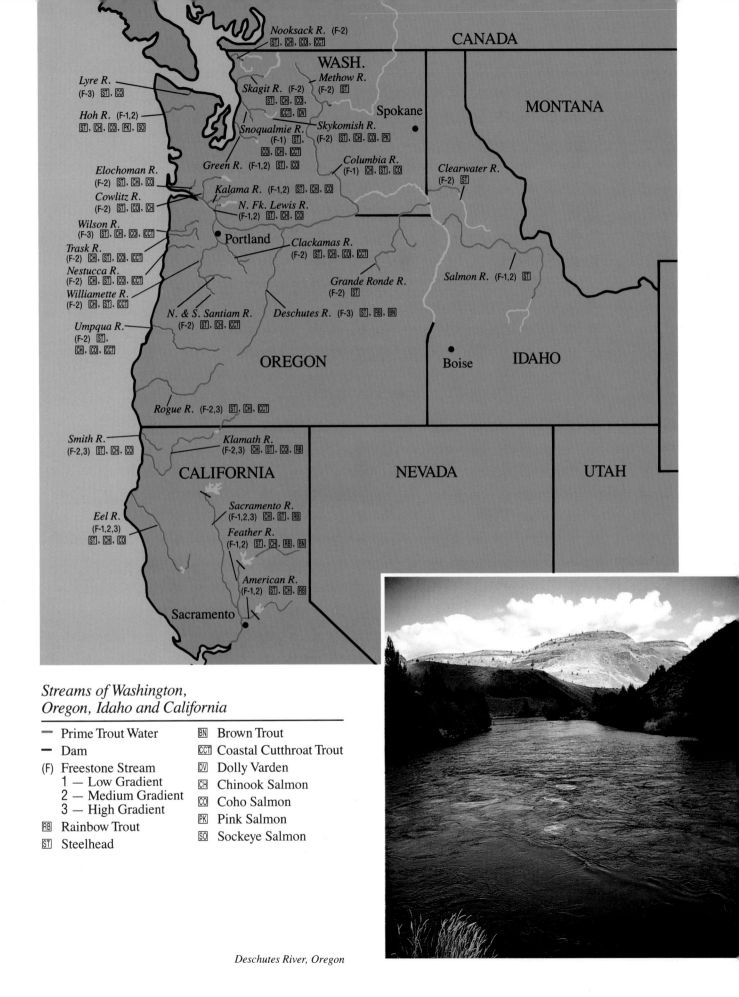

Nooksack R. (F-2)
ST, CH, CO, CCT

Lyre R.
(F-3) ST, CO

Hoh R. (F-1,2)
ST, CH, CO, PK, SO

Elochoman R.
(F-2) ST, CH, CO

Cowlitz R.
(F-2) ST, CO, CH

Wilson R.
(F-3) ST, CH, CO, CCT

Trask R.
(F-2) CH, ST, CO, CCT

Nestucca R.
(F-2) CH, ST, CO, CCT

Williamette R.
(F-2) CH, ST, CCT

Umpqua R.
(F-2) ST,
CH, CO, CCT

Smith R.
(F-2,3) ST, CH, CO

Eel R.
(F-1,2,3)
ST, CH, CO

CANADA

WASH.

Methow R.
(F-2) ST

Skagit R. (F-2)
ST, CH, CO,
CCT, DV

Spokane

Snoqualmie R.
(F-1) ST,
CO, CH, CCT

Skykomish R.
(F-2) ST, CH, CO, PK

Green R. (F-1,2) ST, CO

Columbia R.
(F-1) CH, ST, CO

Kalama R. (F-1,2) ST, CH, CO

N. Fk. Lewis R.
(F-1,2) ST, CH, CO

Portland

Clackamas R.
(F-2) ST, CH, CO, CCT

Grande Ronde R.
(F-2) ST

N. & S. Santiam R.
(F-2) ST, CH, CCT

Deschutes R. (F-3) ST, RB, BN

OREGON

Rogue R. (F-2,3) ST, CH, CCT

Klamath R.
(F-2,3) CH, ST, CO, RB

CALIFORNIA

Sacramento R.
(F-1,2,3) CH, ST, RB

Feather R.
(F-1,2) ST, CH, RB, BN

American R.
(F-1,2) ST, CH, RB

Sacramento

MONTANA

Clearwater R.
(F-2) ST

Salmon R. (F-1,2) ST

Boise

IDAHO

NEVADA

UTAH

Streams of Washington,
Oregon, Idaho and California

— Prime Trout Water
▬ Dam
(F) Freestone Stream
  1 — Low Gradient
  2 — Medium Gradient
  3 — High Gradient
RB Rainbow Trout
ST Steelhead

BN Brown Trout
CCT Coastal Cutthroat Trout
DV Dolly Varden
CH Chinook Salmon
CO Coho Salmon
PK Pink Salmon
SO Sockeye Salmon

Deschutes River, Oregon

153

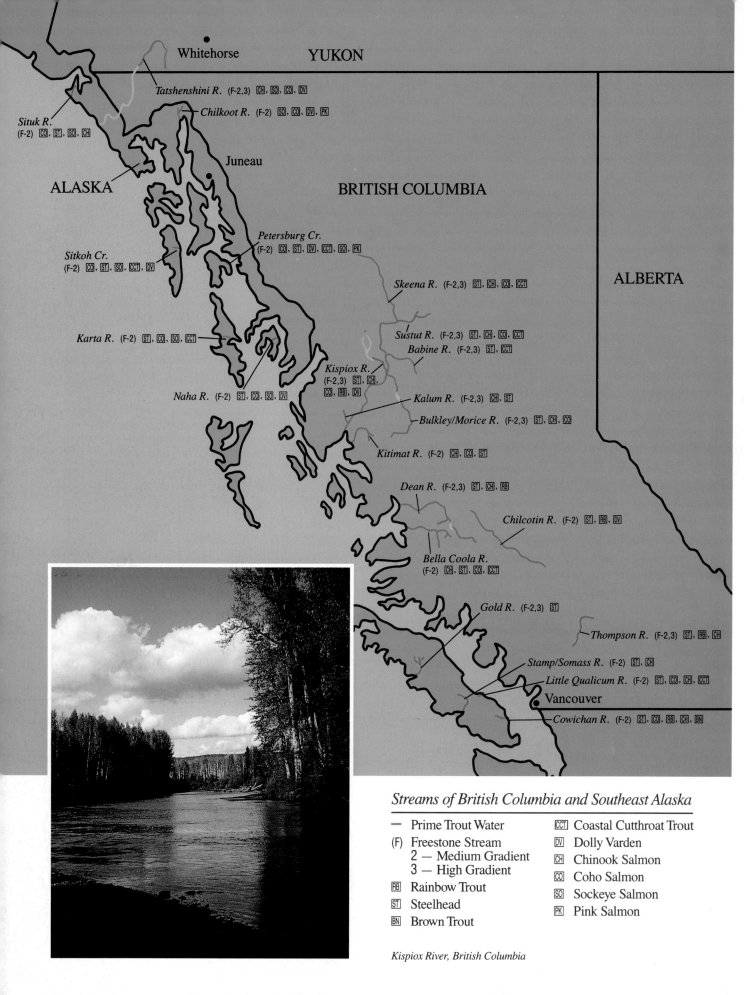

Whitehorse **YUKON**

Tatshenshini R. (F-2,3) CH, SO, CO, DV

Chilkoot R. (F-2) SO, CO, DV, PK

Situk R.
(F-2) CO, ST, SO, CH

Juneau

ALASKA

BRITISH COLUMBIA

ALBERTA

Petersburg Cr.
(F-2) CO, ST, DV, CCT, SO, PK

Sitkoh Cr.
(F-2) CO, ST, SO, CCT, DV

Skeena R. (F-2,3) ST, CH, CO, CCT

Karta R. (F-2) ST, CO, SO, CCT

Sustut R. (F-2,3) ST, CH, CO, CCT

Babine R. (F-2,3) ST, CCT

Kispiox R.
(F-2,3) ST, CH,
CO, RB, DV

Naha R. (F-2) ST, CO, SO, DV

Kalum R. (F-2,3) CH, ST

Bulkley/Morice R. (F-2,3) ST, CH, CO

Kitimat R. (F-2) CH, CO, ST

Dean R. (F-2,3) ST, CH, RB

Chilcotin R. (F-2) ST, RB, DV

Bella Coola R.
(F-2) CH, ST, CO, CCT

Gold R. (F-2,3) ST

Thompson R. (F-2,3) ST, RB, CH

Stamp/Somass R. (F-2) ST, CH

Little Qualicum R. (F-2) ST, CO, CH, CCT

Vancouver

Cowichan R. (F-2) ST, CO, RB, CH, BN

Streams of British Columbia and Southeast Alaska

— Prime Trout Water
(F) Freestone Stream
  2 — Medium Gradient
  3 — High Gradient
RB Rainbow Trout
ST Steelhead
BN Brown Trout

CCT Coastal Cutthroat Trout
DV Dolly Varden
CH Chinook Salmon
CO Coho Salmon
SO Sockeye Salmon
PK Pink Salmon

Kispiox River, British Columbia

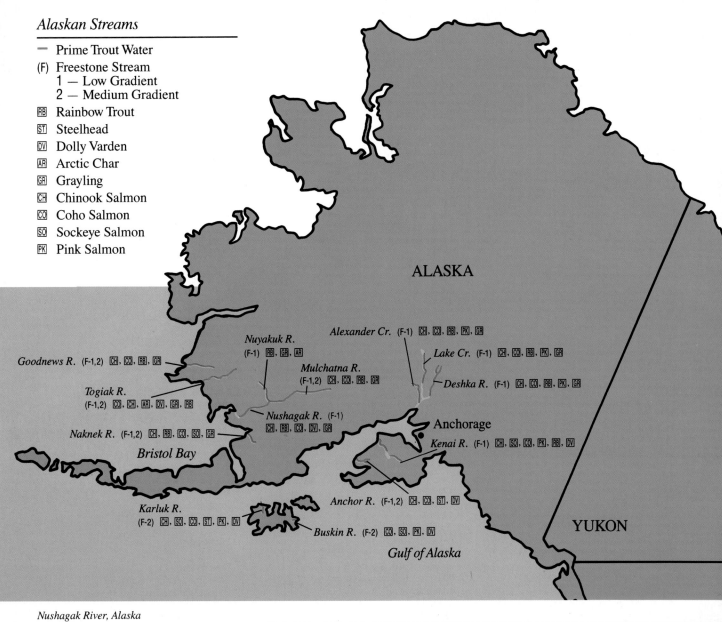

Alaskan Streams

— Prime Trout Water

(F) Freestone Stream
    1 — Low Gradient
    2 — Medium Gradient

RB Rainbow Trout

ST Steelhead

DV Dolly Varden

AR Arctic Char

GR Grayling

CH Chinook Salmon

CO Coho Salmon

SO Sockeye Salmon

PK Pink Salmon

ALASKA

YUKON

Alexander Cr. (F-1) CH, CO, RB, PK, GR

Lake Cr. (F-1) CH, CO, RB, PK, GR

Nuyakuk R. (F-1) RB, GR, AR

Mulchatna R. (F-1,2) CH, CO, RB, GR

Deshka R. (F-1) CH, CO, RB, PK, GR

Goodnews R. (F-1,2) CH, CO, RB, GR

Togiak R. (F-1,2) CO, CH, AR, DV, GR, RB

Nushagak R. (F-1) CH, RB, CO, DV, GR

Anchorage

Naknek R. (F-1,2) CH, RB, CO, SO, GR

Kenai R. (F-1) CH, SO, CO, PK, RB, DV

Bristol Bay

Anchor R. (F-1,2) CH, CO, ST, DV

Karluk R. (F-2) CH, SO, CO, ST, PK, DV

Buskin R. (F-2) CO, SO, PK, DV

Gulf of Alaska

Nushagak River, Alaska

Index